Dear Reader,

Anyone who wishes to understand how Unitarian Universalist churches function ought to begin with a study of the Cambridge Platform, a document signed in 1648. As different as Unitarian Universalists are in theology from members of other congregationally ordered churches, they share a common tradition of polity that originated with this document. Based entirely on Biblical interpretation, the signers of the Cambridge Platform set forth basic principles about how to define membership, choose leaders, come to decisions, handle dissent, and act together despite disagreements.

The Cambridge Platform is both a declaration of religious independence and an ecclesiastical constitution, adopted well over a century before the corresponding political documents that marked the founding of the United States of America. Derived from British Protestant practice but differing from it in crucial detail, the Platform established a non-hierarchical congregational polity, meaning that churches would be independent both of outside authority and of each other. The later Congregationalist and Unitarian denominations evolved from the early New England churches governed by the Platform. Universalists were also ordered by Congregational polity. Because of this, when the Unitarians and Universalists consolidated in 1961 to form the Unitarian Universalist Association, they adopted a polity greatly indebted to the Cambridge Platform.

This book presents the Cambridge Platform to a new generation of ministers and laypeople interested in the origin of the way things are done in our churches today. This edition features an introduction by Alice Blair Wesley that provides historical context for the Cambridge Platform and explores the regard that its framers held for the Bible as their source of religious authority. The historical document itself has been edited for improved readability, with modernized spelling and punctuation but no changes to the original content. I have also corrected errors and reconciled inconsistencies in the Biblical citations from other editions of the Platform.

Throughout the Cambridge Platform, its framers continuously reference the Bible as their authority, which makes the Bible a foundational document for the polity of Unitarianism, Universalism, and the other faiths shaped by Puritanism. This edition connects the Biblical citations as specifically as possible to the Platform text, allowing readers to identify the scriptural authority behind each of the principles expressed in the Platform. My hope is that this will allow liberal religious readers to begin to reclaim our biblical heritage. Christian conservatives tend to turn to the Bible as their authority for specific theological belief, but the authors of the Cambridge Platform had a more expansive vision of what scripture had to offer. The ancient words set them on a road to a new kind of religious community, one in which individuals could seek the divine independently and yet continue to walk together.

Peter Hughes

THE
CAMBRIDGE
PLATFORM

CONTEMPORARY READER'S EDITION

Peter Hughes

EDITOR

Skinner House Books

Boston

Printed in the United States

Text design by Jeff Miller

print ISBN: 978-1-55896-537-9
eBook ISBN: 978-1-55896-597-3

6 5 4 3 2
11

Library of Congress Cataloging-in-Publication Data

Cambridge Synod (1646–1648 : Cambridge, Mass.)
    The Cambridge platform : a contemporary reader's edition / Peter Hughes, editor.
        p. cm.
    ISBN-13: 978-1-55896-537-9 (pbk. : alk paper)
    ISBN-10: 1-55896-537-8 (pbk. : alk. paper) 1. Congregational churches—New England—Government. 2. Congregational churches—New England—Discipline. I. Hughes, Peter D., Min. II. Title.

BX7240.C3 2008
262'.058—dc22

                                                                2007051937

CONTENTS

Most Unitarian Universalists have learned that our Universalist and Unitarian ancestors departed from their common Puritan heritage over the doctrines of innate human depravity and the arbitrary salvation of an elect few. But these doctrines were broadly shared among Europe's Protestant reformers at the time. They had nothing to do with the reasons the founders of our oldest churches made the brave and costly choice to cross the Atlantic and settle in a wilderness.

Both the Pilgrims in 1620 and the 20,000 or so Puritans who came to New England in the Great Migration of the 1630s were primarily concerned with a theology of organization: how churches ought to be organized in the spirit of mutual love and who in these churches should have authority and why. They came to gather themselves into free churches "in the liberty of the gospel." (Though the term *free church* was not in use in the 17th century, it aptly designates the Puritan concept of an authentic church.) In so doing, they invented—or rather reinvented—what we call congregational polity, in which each congregation is independent and ecclesiastically sovereign. From their beginnings, American Universalist and Unitarian churches have been congregational in their polity, as are all member congregations of the Unitarian Universalist Association of Congregations today. We have faithfully preserved the most significant part of our Puritan heritage!

English Puritans had tried for decades before the Great Migration to reform the Church of England in the direction of a more personally experienced spirituality. They were thwarted, persecuted, and punished by the monarchs and bishops of England for holding what we would call study groups and conferences among laity as well as ministers and for public preaching on market days. Eventually the Puritans concluded that something had gone terribly awry in a Church that would not allow such innocent and beneficial gatherings. Their experience led them to look to the Old and New Testaments where they found very different patterns of authority.

These earliest settlers in the Massachusetts Bay hoped that they would be joined by more dissenters from the Church of England, of whom there were many. But the situation in England changed drastically in the 1640s with the outbreak of civil war, the beheading of Charles I, the rule of Parliament, and the rise to power of the Lord Protector, Oliver Cromwell. In that turmoil, there emerged in Cromwell's army passionately religious Puritan advocates for a far more revolutionary economic reorganization of society than England was ready for. Accordingly, opinion concerning church governance, even among those who dissented from Episcopal polity (control of churches by a hierarchy of bishops), shifted away from congregationalism toward presbyterianism, a pattern of authority that would give church leaders more power to deal with extremists.

New England Puritans, who located all religious authority in the gathered members of each congregation, were well aware of the shift toward presbyterianism among their friends in England. In 1645, Parliament invited two widely respected New England theologians, John Cotton and Thomas Hooker, to attend the meetings of 109 "divines" and 24 members of Parliament in Westminster Hall in London. The purpose of these meetings was to determine the faith and order of the Church of England—that is, its theology and form of governance. Cotton and Hooker did not go because they knew that they would be in the minority. The assembly subsequently published the Westminster Confession, which prescribed a presbyterial church order.

After the publication of the Westminster Confession, and at the request of the Massachusetts General Court, the New England churches sent elected lay and ministerial officers, or "messengers," to convene in a synod, known as the Cambridge Synod because it met in the Cambridge meetinghouse. This assembly "thought it good to present unto [the local churches], and with them all the churches of Christ abroad, our professed and hearty assent and attestation" to the Westminster Confession, "excepting only some sections" that is, those sections having to do with authority in the church.

The Cambridge Platform explains and justifies how congregational churches work. It is heavily footnoted with references to passages from the Scriptures illustrating the understanding that the substance of the congregational way is the same as that of the very first free church, the family of Sarah and Abraham. For the authors of the Platform, free churches are groups of people who have covenanted to "walk together," as they are called by God to do, in the spirit of mutual love. People have covenanted to do this over a great stretch of time, they pointed out, first as families, beginning with Sarah and Abraham; then as the nation of ancient Israel, beginning with Moses; and since the time of Jesus and his disciples, as local congregations without reference to nationality. These congregationalists understood the Bible to be mainly about the free and covenanted social practice of love. As they understood church history, the "substance" of a free church has always been the same, the holy spirit of mutual love. (That is why they found the Old Testament as instructive as the New.) The living, gathered bodies of the members are the "matter" of the free church. Its "form," the covenantal promise, defines the membership, determines its organizational structure, and imbues the church with promise, the potential to be a life-giving organization in the larger world, "a city set upon a hill" that gives light to all.

According to the Platform, "The parts of church government are all of them exactly described in the word of God being parts or means of instituted worship according to the second commandment, and therefore to continue one and the same unto the appearing of our Lord Jesus Christ." Jesus famously commended a reading of the law in which the "second commandment" is given as "Thou shalt love thy neighbor as thyself." The Platform can be understood to declare that the substance of the free church is the spirit of neighborly love. Everything in its "administration" follows from the primacy of this one experienced, central, holy reality. Elsewhere in the text the spirit of love is called "the supreme power," or Christ, the only "head" of the church. The one end of everything the gathered members do, says the Platform, is "edification," that is, mutual learning and teaching concerning the many and complex ways of love. The people must gather regularly and often for ongoing mutual learning to take place. Otherwise, the "spirit of love" is just a bodiless abstraction.

To gather and go about a church's administration, the members needed to do three things: to experience personally the spirit of mutual love between the individual and God, often described in Puritan sermons as a "marriage of the heart"; to be individually drawn by the spirit to covenant with other members; and to elect lay and ministerial officers. This, they said, is the complete free church, just members and officers. Free churches have no need, in church affairs, of any higher authorities. Or, as they put it, "It is not left in the power of men, officers, churches, or any state in the world, to add, or diminish, or alter any thing in the least measure therein." This formulation does not allow for outside supervision or interference by the civil government, bishops, or any provincial presbyterial body.

In the minds of our congregationalist founders, no desire for separatist isolation followed from their strong convictions about the proper autonomy of each church. They drew from the Bible a concept of the church universal—the "catholic church"—that great measureless company of the elect, the living and the dead of every age and land who have ever experienced and walked in the spirit of mutual love, in whatever church, however "corrupted." They would not make an idol of church organization, even the only one they believed to be right. "Has the Lord indeed left to us such hardness of heart that . . . we cannot leave contesting and contending about it till the kingdom be destroyed?" they asked.

These lines demonstrate that strong-minded congregationalists could certainly see the need for, and plead for, tolerance. The authors insisted they were not "separatists." They also insisted that the autonomy of free churches did not imply isolation from other free churches. Though all their churches were "distinct . . . and therefore have no dominion one over another," they were to be a community of independent churches. They were to take thought for one another's welfare. "When any church wants light or peace amongst themselves, it is a way of communion . . . to meet together . . . to consider and argue the points in doubt or difference and, having found out the way of truth and peace, to commend the same . . . to the churches whom the same may concern."

Thus, when members of a local church were unable to resolve some difference, they asked for a council meeting. On an appointed day, neighboring parishes each sent leaders, lay and ordained, to meet with the troubled church and hear all sides of the dispute. The council then offered non-binding advice, which was usually accepted. On rare occasions, church leaders met in formal synods. Conclusions of a synod, like those of the councils, were merely advisory until members of a local church voted to adopt them in their own meeting.

It was not acceptable for a church "rent with divisions" to refuse to consult with other churches "for healing." If a divided church refused to consult, neighboring churches were to "exercise a fuller act of brotherly communion . . . by way of admonition." That is, free churches were not to regard the challenging difficulties in congregational life—either their own or others'—as none of anyone else's business. Rather, each was to listen to other churches' counsel. "So may one church admonish another, and yet without usurpation." Early on, because they so feared that some might accrue inordinate influence, the churches would not even let their ministers meet routinely. Yet the congregations often asked for and gave one another help. In 1637, founders of the Dedham Church, for example, sent one or two leaders to learn how other churches had handled various matters before deciding how to establish their own.

For many years, in churches founded by the Puritans, informally arranged pulpit exchanges were common. Ministers often preached in other pulpits than their own. In the mid-1800s, Henry David Thoreau wrote in *A Week on the Concord and Merrimack Rivers* of the "Monday men" going home after pulpit exchanges: "They cross each other's routes all the country over like warp and woof, making a garment of loose texture. . . ." But long before the onset of frequent pulpit exchanges, lay members wove the institutional garment well. They went to Thursday lectures in other churches than their own, which were often followed by hours of discussion. Lay members also attended morning and afternoon Sunday services when they visited friends, as they often did for a week or even a season.

In all times it is a good thing, says the Platform, if all the members of two or several churches occasionally come together. A church with two ministers should lend one to a congregation whose minister is ill. When members move, even temporarily, to another town, the church should send a letter of recommendation to the congregation in that town. In case of need, one church should furnish another with officers or money. And neighboring churches should help a new church get started well. If any church gets too large to meet all in one place, some of the members should form a new congregation, "as bees, when the hive is too full, issue forth by swarms and are gathered into other hives."

Thus, with no hierarchy, but with well-used lateral patterns of engagement, the churches influenced and helped each other substantially. These institutional patterns, by their very design, both allowed scrupulous respect for each congregation's independence and encouraged effective cooperation.

Did the congregationalists really get all this from the Bible? They thought so. They read the Bible with a special interpretive key, asking of the texts, "What was decided here? Who decided? Whose counsel was offered, even if unasked? Which people had to be involved if a decision was to be considered legitimate? What did people in these stories do if they disagreed?" They then inferred that answers to these questions illustrated the "rules" of authentic authority in free churches.

For example, though the office did not long survive in practice, the Platform said each church should elect a "ruling elder." This officer would speak privately and tenderly but firmly with any member whose behavior was at odds with the spirit of love. If the member refused to listen and still refused, even when two or three other members were called in, the ruling elder took the issue to the whole church. All the members together decided whether a reprimand or dismissal was in order. The ruling elder could not pronounce by himself on any issue; authentic authority lay in the whole gathered congregation. This model for both the office and the limited power of the ruling elder was based on one of Jesus' sermons in the Gospel according to Matthew.

But discipline was not solely the ruling elder's responsibility. Every member was expected to speak candidly to any member whose ways were unloving. This rule they inferred from a story in the book of Acts. Paul, though he had no authority over Peter, told Peter, in front of the whole church, that it was wrong of him to refuse to eat with Gentile members at church suppers.

For all its framers' reverence for the Scriptures, the Platform includes a rather impatient-sounding admission that not every "necessary circumstance" of the free church is clearly indicated by a biblical passage. If any procedures should seem only practical or necessary, two tests of reason were to be applied: Is their end "unto edification"? And are they done "decently and in order, according to the nature of the things themselves, and civil and church custom"?

The Platform goes on to argue, "Does not even nature itself teach you? Yea, they are in some sort determined particularly. . . . So as, if there be no error of man concerning their determination, the determining of them is to be accounted as if it were divine."

Our congregational founders made what we can only call mistakes, in hindsight, that were costly to later generations by adopting precisely those patterns "accounted as if . . . divine," when they were merely habits "of civil and church custom" brought from Europe. They were bad habits, not because Bible stories contain no precedent for them, but because they would work ill in the long run, determined as they were, not in the spirit of mutual love, but by familiar patterns of authoritarian coercion.

Money was certainly necessary for churches, which served their entire towns, later called "parishes." Early congregationalists thought it perfectly reasonable that the magistrates, as they had done in England, should coerce all landowning citizens to pay the parish tax to support free churches—those churches properly constituted according to the Cambridge Platform. In 1692 the General Court enacted a law to that effect. The law never forbade the organization of other kinds of churches. However, members of other churches would later have great difficulty getting an exemption from paying the parish tax that supported the legally designated free churches.

The congregational founders made another mistake in setting forth the criteria for membership. Early in the text, the Cambridge Platform makes a very strong statement on the importance of covenant. Only each member's promise, made freely and individually, to walk together with other members in the ways of love makes the people a free church. The Platform reads:

This form then being by mutual covenant, it follows, it is not faith in the heart, nor the profession of that faith, nor cohabitation, nor baptism.

1. Not faith in the heart, because that is invisible.

2. Not a bare profession, because that declares them no more to be members of one church than of another.

3. Not cohabitation: atheists or infidels may dwell together with believers.

4. Not baptism, because it presupposes a church estate . . . the church being before it, and in the wilderness without it.

But then in Chapter XII, titled "Of Admission of Members into the Church," the Platform says, "Such as are admitted thereto as members ought to be examined and tried first, whether they be fit and meet to be received." And further on, "They must profess and hold forth in such sort as may satisfy rational charity that [repentance and faith] are there indeed." And again, "A personal and public confession and declaring of God's manner of working upon the soul is both lawful, expedient, and useful in sundry respects and upon sundry grounds."

The insistence that old members test and judge the substance of new members' neighborly love was a serious mistake. It soon gave the founders and generations of their heirs no end of trouble. The founders had tied entering the covenant to a particular kind of experience, an ecstatic "falling in love with God," that they thought distinguished the converted elect and that applicants for membership should be willing and able to describe. But most of the founders' own children never had that experience, or if they did, they seldom volunteered publicly to describe it. (Many congregations adopted the "Half-way Covenant" so that the babies of as yet unregenerate parents could be baptized.) By the eighteenth-century preachers like Jonathan Edwards and other revivalists came to believe they could induce the qualifying conversion experience through fear. Over time, then, entering a church covenant became linked in liberals' minds with orthodoxy and hell-fire preaching. Thus, even though nineteenth-century liberal churches kept the earliest covenants on the books—beautiful, simple promises to walk together in the ways of love—the covenants were largely ignored and not spoken of, a pattern that continued for many decades.

But if one does not speak of the covenant that constitutes the community as a church, the promise that all are cordially invited to enter, then what does one say is the basis of a liberal church? Long experience teaches that it cannot be a creed. I hope the day comes when many can explain, "Ours is a covenantal church. We join by promising one another that we will be a beloved community, meeting together often to find the ways of love, as best we can see to do. We have found there is always more to learn about how love really works, and could work, in our lives and in the world."

The founders also mistakenly assumed that tiered levels of privilege and authority in society, and in the churches, were natural. The Platform said the free church had a "mixed government." "Kingship" of the holy spirit of Christ made the free church a monarchy. And because the members elected and could dismiss their own officers, the free church was a democracy. But then, since the members were to obey their elected officers, the church was also an aristocracy. In actuality, members did not heed dictates with which they disagreed, no matter how often they were admonished.

Nearly all colonial and later New Englanders—of all classes—assumed that any acquired status should be respected in perpetuity. Thus a pattern developed early that lasted in Unitarian churches—and in the AUA and UUA—into the late twentieth century. Ministers and elected lay leaders, unless they did something awful, tended to stay in office for decades. The same was true of civil offices in New England towns and in the legislature. Connections and influence often led to inherited wealth. So rather quickly, New England developed something like a European aristocracy, a class economically and politically privileged by birth. Many nineteenth-century Unitarians were of this class, directly benefiting from old patterns of privilege. There are advantages to a culture in having a well-educated and wealthy class, but in the long run patterns of assumed privilege lead to complacency. Established authority figures do not like change and will resist it mightily, even when it is needed.

Courageous, intelligent, and creative though they were, the seventeenth-century congregationalists failed to see the consequences of mistaken assumptions. They rightly saw as divine gifts the love in their hearts and the human capacity to reason about and learn together the ways of love. Yet they also believed it was fine to take their reasoning about practical, "necessary circumstances" as divine "if there be no error"! A rather large "if," one might say. But if the Platform authors were overconfident that they could find the truth with close enough attention to logic and rules, we need to remember that, in this, they were at one with the spirit of their age. The seventeenth century was a time of great scientific discovery. Doctrinaire belief in certain circles held that the logical, mathematical discoveries of Newton heralded our coming acquisition of the absolute truth about everything. The Puritans were not the only ones in their time, or later, to be too sure of themselves.

How much more, then, do we need to remind ourselves that unrecognized and false assumptions, characteristic of our time, must be part of who we are as well. It is arrogant to belittle or demonize the generations before us for the mistakes that we can see with the benefit of hindsight. To understand ourselves, we need to be as clear as we can about their gifts to us as well as their mistakes, because the consequences of both have shaped us. We can then consider anew what reclaimed patterns of governance might be good for us, especially in our ways of associating as liberal free congregations. Like our congregational forebears, we need to reflect on what new patterns, based in the spirit of neighborly love, may be appropriate for our time and society.

Alice Blair Wesley

THE CAMBRIDGE PLATFORM

A Platform of Church Discipline, Gathered Out of the Word of God, and Agreed upon by the Elders and Messengers of the Churches Assembled in the Synod at Cambridge in New England, to Be Presented to the Churches and General Court for their Consideration and Acceptance in the Lord, the Eighth Month, Anno 1649.

How amiable are thy tabernacles, O Lord of hosts!
PSALM 84.1

Lord, I have loved the habitation of thy house, and the place where thine honor dwelleth. PSALM 26.8

One thing I have desired of the Lord, that will I seek after; that I may dwell in the house of the Lord all the days of my life, to behold the beauty of the Lord, and to inquire in his temple. PSALM 27.4

THE PREFACE

The setting forth of the public confession of the faith of churches has a double end, and both tending to public edification. First, the maintenance of the faith entire within itself; secondly, the holding forth of unity and harmony, both amongst and with other churches. Our churches here, as, by the grace of Christ, we believe and profess the same doctrine of the truth of the gospel which generally is received in all the reformed churches of Christ in Europe; so especially we desire not to vary from the doctrine of faith and truth held forth by the churches of our native country. For, though it be not one native country that can breed us all of one mind, nor ought we for to have the glorious faith of our Lord Jesus with respect of persons, yet as Paul, who was himself a Jew, professed to hold forth the doctrine of justification by faith and of the resurrection of the dead, according as he knew his godly countrymen did who were Jews by nature,[1] so we, who are by nature Englishmen, do desire to hold forth the same doctrine of religion, especially in fundamentals, which we see and know to be held by the churches of England, according to the truth of the gospel.

The more we discern—that which we do and have cause to do with incessant mourning and trembling—the unkind, and unbrotherly, and unchristian contentions of our godly brethren and countrymen in matters of church government, the more earnestly do we desire to see them joined together in one common faith and ourselves with them. For this end, having pursued the public confession of faith agreed upon by the reverend assembly of divines at Westminster, and finding the sum and substance thereof, in matters of doctrine, to express not their own judgments only, but ours also, and being likewise called upon by our godly magistrates to draw up a public confession of that faith which is constantly taught and generally professed amongst us, we thought good to present unto them, and with them to our churches, and with them to all the churches of Christ abroad, our professed and hearty assent and attestation to the whole confession of faith—for substance of doctrine—which the reverend assembly presented to the religious and honorable Parliament of England, excepting only some sections in the 25th, 30th, and 31st chapters of their confession, which concern points of controversy in church discipline, touching which we refer ourselves to the draft of church discipline in the ensuing treatise.

The truth of what we here declare may appear, by the unanimous vote of the Synod of the Elders and messengers of our churches assembled at Cambridge, the last of the sixth month, 1648, which jointly passed in these words: "This Synod, having perused and considered (with much gladness of heart and thankfulness to God) the confession of faith published of late by the reverend assembly in England, do judge it to be very holy, orthodox, and judicious in all matters of faith; and do, therefore, freely and fully consent thereunto for the substance thereof. Only in those things which have respect to church government and discipline, we refer ourselves to the platform of church discipline agreed upon by this present assembly; and do therefore think it meet that this confession of faith should be commended to the churches of Christ among us and to the honored Court as worthy of their due consideration and acceptance." Howbeit, we may not conceal that the doctrine of vocation expressed in chapter 10, section 1, and summarily repeated in chapters 13 and 1, passed not without some debate. Yet considering that the term of vocation, and others by which it is described, are capable of a large or more strict sense and use, and that it is not intended to bind apprehensions precisely in point of order or method, there has been a general condescendancy thereunto.

Now, by this our professed consent and free concurrence with them in all the doctrines of religion, we hope it may appear to the world that as we are a remnant of the people of the same nation with them, so we are professors of the same common faith and fellow heirs of the same common salvation. Yea moreover, as this our profession of the same faith with them will exempt us, even in their judgments, from suspicion of heresy, so we trust it may exempt us in the like sort from suspicion of schism. That, though we are forced to dissent from them in matters of church discipline, yet our dissent is not taken up out of arrogance of spirit in ourselves, whom they see willingly condescend to learn of them, neither is it carried with uncharitable censoriousness towards them, both which are the proper and essential characters of schism, but in meekness of wisdom, as we walk along with them and follow them, as they follow Christ. So, where we conceive a different apprehension of the mind of Christ, as it falls out in some few points touching church order, we still reserve due reverence to them, whom we judge to be, through Christ, the glorious lights of both nations, and only crave leave, as in spirit we are bound, to follow the Lamb wherever he goes. And, after the Apostle's example, as we believe, so we speak.

And if the example of such poor outcasts as ourselves might prevail, if not with all—for that were too great a blessing to hope for— yet with some or other of our brethren in England, so far as they are come to mind and speak the same thing with such as dissent from them, we hope in Christ it would not only moderate the harsh judging and condemning of one another in such differences of judgment, as may be found in the choicest saints, but also prevent, by the mercy of Christ, the peril of the distraction and destruction of all the churches in both kingdoms. Otherwise, if brethren shall go on to bite and devour one another, the Apostle feared, as we also with sadness of heart do, it will tend to the consuming of them and us all, which the Lord prevent.

We are not ignorant that, besides these aspersions of heresy and schism, other exceptions also are taken at our way of church government; but, as we conceive, upon as little ground.

As 1. That, by admitting none into the fellowship of our church but saints by calling, we rob many parish churches of their best members to make up one of our congregations, which is not only to gather churches out of churches (a thing unheard of in Scripture), but also to weaken the hearts and hands of the best ministers in the parishes by despoiling them of their best hearers.

2. That we provide no course for the gaining and calling in of ignorant and erroneous and scandalous persons, whom we refuse to receive into our churches and so exclude from the wholesome remedy of church discipline.

3. That, in our way, we sow seeds of division and hindrance of edification in every family. While admitting into our churches only voluntaries, the husband will be of one church, the wife of

another; the parents of one church, the children of another; the master of one church, the servants of another. And so the parents and masters being of different churches from their children and servants, they cannot take a just account of their profiting by what they hear. Yea, by this means the husbands, parents, and masters shall be chargeable to the maintenance of many other churches and church officers besides their own, which will prove a charge and burden unsupportable.

But for answer as to the first: For gathering churches out of churches, we cannot say that is a thing unheard of in Scripture. The first Christian church was gathered out of the Jewish church, and out of many synagogues in that church, and consisted partly of the inhabitants of Jerusalem, partly of the Galileans, who though they kept some communion in some parts of public worship with the temple, yet neither did they frequent the sacrifices nor repair to the Sanhedrin for the determining of their church causes, but kept entire and constant communion with the Apostles' church in all the ordinances of the gospel. And, for the first Christian church of the gentiles at Antioch, it appears to have been gathered and constituted partly of the dispersed brethren of the church at Jerusalem (whereof some were men of Cyprus and Cyrene) and partly of the believing gentiles.[2]

If it be said the first Christian church at Jerusalem and that at Antioch were gathered not out of any Christian church, but out of the Jewish temple and synagogues, which were shortly after to be abolished, and their gathering to Antioch was upon occasion of dispersion in time of persecution, we desire it may be considered,

1. That the members of the Jewish church were more strongly and straightly tied by express holy covenant to keep fellowship with the Jewish church, till it was abolished, than any members of Christian parish churches are wont to be tied to keep fellowship with their parish churches. The episcopal canons, which bind them to attend on their parish church, it is likely they are now abolished with the episcopacy. The common law of the land is satisfied (as we conceive) if they attend upon the worship of God in any other church, though not within their own parish. But no such like covenant of God, nor any other religious tie, lies upon them to attend the worship of God in

their own parish church as it did lie upon the Jews to attend upon the worship of God in their Temple and synagogues.

2. Though the Jewish temple church at Jerusalem was to be abolished, yet that does not make the desertion of it by the members to be lawful till it was abolished. Future abolition is no warrant for present desertion, unless it be lawful in some case whilst the church is yet in present standing to desert it: to wit, either for avoiding of present pollutions or for hope of greater edification, and so for better satisfaction to conscience in either. Future events, or foresight of them, do not dissolve present relations. Else wives, children, servants, might desert their husbands, parents, masters, when they be mortally sick.

3. What the members of the Jewish church did, in joining to the church at Antioch in time of persecution, it may well be conceived the members of any Christian church may do the like for satisfaction of conscience. Peace of conscience is more desirable than the peace of the outward man and freedom from scruples of conscience is more comfortable to a sincere heart than freedom from persecution.

If it be said these members of the Christian church at Jerusalem that joined to the church at Antioch removed their habitations together with their relations, which, if the brethren of the congregational way would do, it would much abate the grievance of their departure from their presbyterial churches, we verily could wish them so to do, as well approving the like removal of habitations in case of changing church relations, provided that it may be done without too much detriment to their outward estates, and we for our parts have done the same. But, to put a necessity of removal of habitation in such a case, it is to foment and cherish a corrupt principle of making civil cohabitation, if not a formal cause yet at least a proper adjunct of church-relation, which the truth of the gospel does not acknowledge. Now to foment an error to the prejudice of the truth of the gospel is not to walk with a right foot according to the truth of the gospel, as Paul judges.[3]

4. We do not think it meet or safe for a member of a presbyterial church forthwith to desert his relation to his church, betake himself to the fellowship of a congregational church, though he may discern some defect in the estate or government of his own.

For 1. Faithfulness of brotherly love in church relation requires that the members of the church should first convince their brethren of their sinful defects and duly wait for their reformation before they depart from them. For, if we must take such a course for the healing of a private brother in a way of brotherly love, with much meekness and patience, how much more ought we so to walk with like tenderness towards a whole church.

Again 2. By the hasty departure of sound members from a defective church, reformation is not promoted, but many times retarded and corruption increased. Whereas, on the contrary, while sincere members breathing after purity of reformation abide together, they may, by the blessing of God upon their faithful endeavors, prevail much with their elders and neighbors towards a reformation. It may be so much as that their elders in their own church shall receive none to the seals but visible saints and in the classis shall put forth no authoritative act, but consultative only, touching the members of other churches, nor touching their own, but with the consent—silent consent at least—of their own church; which two things, if they can obtain with any humble, meek, holy, faithful endeavors, we conceive they might, by the grace of Christ, find liberty of conscience to continue their relation with their own presbyterial church without scruple.

5. But to add a word farther touching the gathering of churches out of churches: what if there were no express example of such a thing extant in the Scriptures? That which we are wont to answer the Anti-paedobaptists may suffice here—it is enough, if any evidence thereof may be gathered from just consequence of Scripture light. Dr. Ames's judgment concerning this case passes (for aught we know) without exception, which he gave in his 4th book *Of Conscience* in answer to Question 3, C. 24.[4]

"If any," says he, "wronged with unjust vexation or providing for his own edification or in testimony against sin, depart from a church where some evils are tolerated and join himself to another more pure, yet without condemning of the church he leaves, he is not therefore to be held as a schismatic or as guilty of any other sin." Where the Tripartite disjunction, which the judicious Doctor puts, declares the lawfulness of the departure of a church member from his church—when, either through weariness of unjust vexation or in way of provision for his own edification or in testimony against sin, he joins himself to another congregation more reformed—any one of these he judges a just and lawful cause of departure, though all of them do not concur together. Neither will such a practice despoil the best ministers of the parishes of their best hearers.

For 1. Sometimes the ministers themselves are willing to join with their better sort of hearers in this way of reformation and then they and their hearers continue still their church relation together, yea, and confirm it more straightly and strongly by an express renewed covenant, though the ministers may still continue their wonted preaching to the whole parish.

2. If the ministers do dislike the way of those whom they otherwise count their best members and so refuse to join with them therein, yet, if those members can produce some other ministers to join with them in their own way and still continue their dwelling together in the same town, they may easily order the times of public assembly as to attend constantly upon the ministry of their former church and, either after or before the public assembly of the parish, take an opportunity to gather together for the administration of sacraments and censures and other church ordinances amongst themselves. The first apostolic church assembled to hear the word with the Jewish church in the open courts of the temple, but afterwards gathered together for breaking of bread and other acts of church-order from house to house.

3. Suppose presbyterial churches should communicate some of their best gifted members towards the erecting and gathering of another church. It would not forthwith be their detriment, but may be their enlargement. It is the most noble and perfect work of a living creature, both in nature and grace, to propagate and multiply his kind. And it is the honor of the faithful spouse of Christ, to set forward the work of Christ, as well abroad as at home. The church, to help forward her little sister church, was willing to part with her choice materials, even beams of cedar and such precious living stones as were fit to build a silver palace.[5] In the same book, the church is compared sometime to a

garden, sometime to an orchard.[6] No man plants a garden or orchard, but seeks to get the choicest herbs and plants of his neighbors. And they freely impart them. Nor do they count it a spoil to their gardens and orchards, but rather a glory. Nevertheless, we go not so far: we neither seek nor ask the choice members of the parishes, but accept them being offered.

If it be said, they are not offered by the ministers nor by the parish churches, who have most right in them, but only by themselves.

It may justly be demanded what right or what power have either the ministers or parish church over them? Not by solemn church covenant: for that, though it be the firmest engagement, is not owned, but rejected. If it be by their joining with the parish in the calling and election of a minister to such a congregation at his first coming, there is indeed just weight in such an engagement. Nor do we judge it safe for such to remove from such a minister, unless it be upon such grounds as may justly give him due satisfaction. But if the union of such members to a parish church, and to the ministry thereof, be only by cohabitation within the precincts of the parish, that union, as it was founded upon human law, so by human law it may easily be released. Or, otherwise, if a man remove his habitation, he removes also the bond of his relation and the ground of offense.

4. It need not to be feared that all the best hearers of the best ministers—no, nor the most of them—will depart from them upon point of church government. Those who have found the presence and power of the spirit of Christ breathing in their ministers, either to their conversion or edification, will be slow to change such a ministry of faith and holiness for the liberty of church order. Upon which ground, and sundry other such like, there be doubtless sundry godly and judicious hearers in many parishes in England that do and will prefer their relation to their ministers, though in a presbyterial way, above the congregational confederation.

5. But if all, or the most part of the best hearers of the best ministers of parishes, should depart from them, as preferring in their judgments, the congregational way: yet, in case the congregational way should prove to be of Christ, it will never grieve the

holy hearts of godly ministers, that their hearers should follow after Christ: yea many of themselves (upon due deliberation) will be ready to go along with them. It never grieved nor troubled John Baptist, that his best disciples departed from him to follow after Christ.[7] But in case the congregational way should prove to be, not the institution of Christ (as we take it) but the invention of men: then doubtless, the presbyterial form, if it be of God, will swallow up the other, as Moses's rod devoured the rods of the Egyptians. Nor will this put a necessity upon both the opposite parties, to shift for themselves, and to seek to supplant one another: but only, it will call upon them 'αληθεύεν 'εν 'αγάπη to seek and to follow the truth in love, to attend in faithfulness each unto his own flock, and to administer to them all the holy things of God, and their portion of food in due season: and as for others, quietly to forbear them, and yet to instruct them with meekness that are contrary minded: leaving it to Christ (in the use of all good means) to reveal his own truth in his own time: and meanwhile endeavoring to keep the unity of the Spirit in the bond of peace.[8]

To the 2nd exception, that we "take no course for the gaining and healing and calling in of ignorant and erroneous and scandalous persons, whom we refuse to receive into our churches and so exclude them from the remedy of church discipline":

We conceive the receiving of them into our churches would rather loose and corrupt our churches than gain and heal them. A little leaven laid in a lump of dough will sooner leaven the whole lump than the whole lump will sweeten it. We therefore find it safer to square rough and unhewn stones before they be laid into the building, rather than to hammer and hew them when they lie unevenly in the building.

And, accordingly, two means we use to gain and call in such as are ignorant or scandalous: 1. The public ministry of the word, upon which they are invited by counsel and required by wholesome laws to attend. And the word it is, which is the power of God to salvation, to the calling and winning of souls. 2. Private conference and conviction by the elders and other able brethren of the church, whom they do the more respectively hearken unto when they see no hope of enjoying church fellowship or participation in the sacraments for themselves or their children till they approve their judgments to be sound and orthodox and their lives subdued to some hope of godly conversation. What can classical discipline or excommunication itself do more in this case?

The 3rd exception wraps up in it a threefold domestical inconvenience—and each of them meet to be eschewed: 1. Disunion in families between each relation; 2. Disappointment of edification, for want of opportunity in the governors of families to take account of things heard by their children and servants; 3. Disbursements of chargeable maintenance to the several churches, whereto the several persons of their families are joined.

All which inconveniences either do not fall out in congregational churches or are easily redressed. For none are orderly admitted into congregational churches but such as are well-approved by good testimony to be duly observant of family relations. Or if any otherwise disposed should creep in, they are either orderly healed or duly removed in a way of Christ. Nor are they admitted unless they can give some good account of their profiting by ordinances before the elders and brethren of the church—and much more to their parents, and masters. Godly tutors in the university can take an account of their pupils and godly householders in the city can take account of their children and servants, how they profit by the word they have heard in several churches and that to the greater edification of the whole family by the variety of such administrations. Bees may bring honey and wax into the hive when they are not limited to one garden of flowers but may fly abroad to many.

Nor is any charge expected from wives, children, or servants to the maintenance of congregational churches further than they be furnished with personal estates or earnings which may enable them to contribute of such things as they have and not of such as they have not. God accepts not robbery for a sacrifice. And though a godly householder may justly take himself bound in conscience to contribute to any such church whereto his wife or children or servants do stand in relation, yet that will not aggravate the burden of his charge, no more than if they were received members of the same church whereto himself is related.

But why do we stand thus long to plead exemptions from exceptions? The Lord help all his faithful servants, whether presbyterial or congregational, to judge and shame ourselves before the Lord for all our former compliances to greater enormities in church government than are to be found either in the congregational or presbyterial way. And then, surely, either the Lord will clear up his own will to us and so frame and subdue us all to one mind and one way,[9] or else we shall learn to bear one another's burdens in a spirit of meekness. It will then doubtless be far from us so to attest the discipline of Christ as to detest the disciples of Christ, so to contend for the seamless coat of Christ as to crucify the living members of Christ, so to divide ourselves about church communion as through breaches to open a wide gap for a deluge of Antichristian and profane malignity to swallow up both church and civil state.

What shall we say more? Is difference about church order become the inlet of all the disorders in the kingdom? Has the Lord indeed left us to such hardness of heart that church government shall become a snare to Zion—as sometimes Moses was to Egypt[10]—that we cannot leave contesting and contending about it till the kingdom be destroyed? Did not the Lord Jesus, when he dedicated his sufferings for his church and his also unto his father, make it his earnest and only prayer for us in this world that we all might be one in him?[11] And is it possible that he, whom the Father heard always,[12] should not have this last, most solemn prayer heard and granted? Or shall it be granted for all the saints elsewhere and not for the saints in England, so that amongst them disunion shall grow even about church union and communion? If it is possible for a little faith, so much as a grain of mustard seed, to remove a mountain, is it not possible for so much strength of faith, as is to be found in all the godly in the kingdom, to remove those images of jealousy and to cast those stumbling-blocks out of the way, which may hinder the free passage of brotherly love amongst brethren? It is true indeed the national covenant does justly engage both parties faithfully to endeavor the utter extirpation of the Antichristian hierarchy and, much more, of all blasphemies, heresies, and damnable errors. Certainly, if the congregational discipline be independent from the inventions of men, is it not much more independent from the delusions of Satan? What fellowship has Christ with Belial? Light with darkness? Truth with error? The faithful Jews needed not the help of the Samaritans, to re-edify the temple of God; yea, they rejected their help when it was offered.[13] And if the congregational way be a way of truth, as we believe, and if the brethren that walk in it be zealous of the truth and hate every false way, as by the rule of their holy discipline they are instructed,[14] then, verily, there is no branch in the national covenant that engages the covenanters to abhor either congregational churches or their way, which, being duly administered, do no less effectively extirpate the Antichristian hierarchy and all blasphemies, heresies, and pernicious errors than the other way of discipline does, which is more generally and publicly received and ratified.

But the Lord Jesus commune with all our hearts in secret. And he, who is the King of his Church, let him be pleased to exercise his kingly power in our spirits that so his kingdom may come into our churches in purity and peace. Amen. Amen.

CHAPTER I

Of the Form of Church Government and that It Is One, Immutable, and Prescribed in the Word of God

1. Ecclesiastical polity, or church government or discipline, is nothing else but that form and order that is to be observed in the church of Christ upon earth, both for the constitution of it, and all the administrations that therein are to be performed.[15]

2. Church government is considered in a double respect, either in regard of the parts of government themselves, or necessary circumstances thereof. The parts of government are prescribed in the word, because the Lord Jesus Christ, the King and Law-giver of his church, is no less faithful in the house of God than was Moses,[16] who from the Lord delivered a form and pattern of government to the children of Israel in the Old Testament;[17] and the holy Scriptures are now also so perfect as they are able to make the man of God perfect, and thoroughly furnished unto every good work; and therefore doubtless to the well ordering of the house of God.[18]

3. The parts of church government are all of them exactly described in the word of God being parts or means of instituted worship according to the second commandment,[19] and therefore to continue one and the same unto the appearing of our Lord Jesus Christ,[20] as a kingdom that cannot be shaken,[21] until he shall deliver it up unto God, even the Father.[22] So that it is not left in the power of men, officers, churches, or any state in the world, to add, or diminish, or alter any thing in the least measure therein.[23]

4. The necessary circumstances, as time and place, etc., belonging unto order and decency, are not so left unto men, as that, under pretense of them, they may thrust their own inventions upon the churches:[24] Being circumscribed in the word with many general limitations, where they are determined in respect of the matter to be neither worship itself, nor circumstances separable from worship.[25] In respect of their

end, they must be done unto edification; in respect of the manner, decently and in order, according to the nature of the things themselves, and civil and church custom.[26] Does not even nature itself teach you?[27] Yea, they are in some sort determined particularly: namely, that they be done in such a manner as, all circumstances considered, is most expedient for edification.[28] So as, if there be no error of man concerning their determination, the determining of them is to be accounted as if it were divine.[29]

CHAPTER II

Of the Nature of the Catholic Church in General, and in Special, of a Particular Visible Church

1. The catholic church is the whole company of those that are elected, redeemed, and in time effectually called from the state of sin and death unto a state of grace and salvation in Jesus Christ.[30]

2. This church is either triumphant or militant. Triumphant, the number of them who are glorified in heaven;[31] militant, the number of them who are conflicting with their enemies upon earth.[32]

3. This militant church is to be considered as invisible and visible. Invisible, in respect of their relation, wherein they stand to Christ as a body unto the head, being united unto him by the spirit of God and faith in their hearts.[33] Visible, in respect of the profession of their faith, in their persons, and in particular churches. And so there may be acknowledged a universal visible church.[34]

4. The members of the militant visible church, considered either as not yet in church order, or as walking according to the church order of the gospel.[35] In order, and so besides the spiritual union and communion common to all believers, they enjoy moreover a union and communion ecclesiastical, political.[36] So we deny a universal visible church.[37]

5. The state of the members of the militant visible church, walking in order, was either before the law, economical, that is, in families;[38] or under the law, national;[39] or since the coming of Christ, only congregational (the term independent, we approve not): therefore neither national, provincial, nor classical.

6. A congregational church is by the institution of Christ a part of the militant visible church,[40] consisting of a company of saints by calling,[41] united into one body by a holy covenant,[42] for the public worship of God,[43] and the mutual edification one of another in the fellowship of the Lord Jesus.[44]

CHAPTER III

Of the Matter of the Visible Church Both in
Respect of Quality and Quantity

1. The matter of a visible church are saints by calling.[45]

2. By saints, we understand,

    I. Such as have not only attained the knowledge of the principles of religion,[46] and are free from gross and open scandals,[47] but also do, together with the profession of their faith and repentance,[48] walk in blameless obedience to the word,[49] so as that in charitable discretion they may be accounted saints by calling (though perhaps some or more of them be unsound and hypocrites inwardly), because the members of such particular churches are commonly by the Holy Ghost called "saints and faithful brethren in Christ";[50] and sundry churches have been reproved for receiving, and suffering such persons to continue in fellowship among them, as have been offensive and scandalous;[51] the name of God also, by this means, is blasphemed, and the holy things of God defiled and profaned,[52] the hearts of the godly grieved, and the wicked themselves hardened and helped forward to damnation.[53] The example of such does endanger the sanctity of others. A little leaven leavens the whole lump.[54]

    II. The children of such, who are also holy.[55]

3. The members of churches, though orderly constituted, may in time degenerate, and grow corrupt and scandalous,[56] which, though they ought not to be tolerated in the church,[57] yet their continuance therein, through the defect of the execution of discipline and just censures, does not immediately dissolve the being of the church, as appears in the church of Israel, and the churches of Galatia and Corinth, Pergamus and Thyatira.[58]

4. The matter of the church, in respect of its quantity, ought not to be of greater number than may ordinarily meet together conveniently in one place;[59] nor ordinarily fewer than may conveniently carry on church work. Hence, when the Holy Scriptures makes mention of the saints combined into a church estate in a town or city, where was but one congregation, it usually calls those saints "the church" in the singular number, as "the church of the Thessalonians," "the church of Smyrna, Philadelphia," and the like;[60] but when it speaks of the saints in a nation or province, wherein there were sundry congregations, it frequently and usually calls them by the name of "churches," in the plural number, as the "churches of Asia, Galatia, Macedonia," and the like;[61] which is further confirmed by what is written of sundry of those churches in particular, how they were assembled and met together the whole church in one place,[62] as the church at Jerusalem, the church at Antioch, the church at Corinth and Cenchrea, though it were more near to Corinth, it being the port thereof, and answerable to a village; yet being a distinct congregation from Corinth, it had a church of its own, as well as Corinth had.[63]

5. Nor can it with reason be thought but that every church appointed and ordained by Christ, had a ministry ordained and appointed for the same; and yet plain it is that there were no ordinary officers appointed by Christ for any other than congregational churches; elders being appointed to feed not all flocks, but the particular flock of God, over which the Holy Ghost had made them the overseers,[64] and that flock they must attend, even the whole flock; and one congregation being as much as any ordinary elders can attend, therefore there is no greater church than a congregation which may ordinarily meet in one place.

CHAPTER IV

Of the Form of a Visible Church
and of Church Covenant

1. Saints by calling must have a visible political union among themselves, or else they are not yet a particular church,[65] as those similitudes hold forth, which Scripture makes use of to show the nature of particular churches; as a body, a building, or house, hands, eyes, feet, and other members,[66] must be united, or else, remaining separate are not a body. Stones, timber, though squared, hewn and polished, are not a house, until they are compacted and united; so saints or believers in judgment of charity, are not a church unless orderly knit together.[67]

2. Particular churches cannot be distinguished one from another but by their forms. Ephesus is not Smyrna, nor Pergamus Thyatira;[68] but each one a distinct society of itself, having officers of their own, which had not the charge of others; virtues of their own, for which others are not praised; corruptions of their own, for which others are not blamed.

3. This form is the visible covenant, agreement, or consent, whereby they give up themselves unto the Lord, to the observing of the ordinances of Christ together in the same society, which is usually called the "church covenant,"[69] for we see not otherwise how members can have church power over one another mutually.[70] The comparing of each particular church to a city, and to a spouse,[71] seems to conclude not only a form, but that that form is by way of a covenant. The covenant, as it was, that which made the family of Abraham and children of Israel to be a church and people unto God,[72] so it is that which now makes the several societies of Gentile believers to be churches in these days.[73]

4. This voluntary agreement, consent, or covenant—for all these are here taken for the same—although the more express and plain it is,

the more fully it puts us in mind of our mutual duty; and stirs us up to it, and leaves less room for the questioning of the truth of the church estate of a company of professors, and the truth of membership of particular persons; yet we conceive the substance of it is kept where there is a real agreement and consent of a company of faithful persons to meet constantly together in one congregation for the public worship of God and their mutual edification; which real agreement and consent they do express by their constant practice in coming together for the public worship of God and by their religious subjection to the ordinances of God there:[74] the rather, if we do consider how Scripture covenants have been entered into, not only expressly by word of mouth, but by sacrifice, by hand writing, and seal; and also sometimes by silent consent, without any writing or expression of words at all.[75]

5. This form then being by mutual covenant, it follows, it is not faith in the heart, nor the profession of that faith, nor cohabitation, nor baptism.

    1. Not faith in the heart, because that is invisible.

    2. Not a bare profession, because that declares them no more to be members of one church than of another.

    3. Not cohabitation: atheists or infidels may dwell together with believers.

    4. Not baptism, because it presupposes a church estate, as circumcision in the Old Testament, which gave no being to the church, the church being before it, and in the wilderness without it. Seals presuppose a covenant already in being. One person is a complete subject of baptism, but one person is incapable of being a church.

6. All believers ought, as God gives them opportunity thereunto, to endeavor to join themselves unto a particular church, and that in respect of the honor of Jesus Christ, in his example and institution, by the professed acknowledgment of and subjection to the order and ordinances of the gospel; as also in respect of their good of communion,[76] founded upon their visible union, and contained in the promises of Christ's special presence in the church; whence they have fellowship with him, and in him, one with another;[77] also for the keeping of them in the way of God's commandments, and recovering of

them in case of wandering, (which all Christ's sheep are subject to in this life), being unable to return of themselves;[78] together with the benefit of their mutual edification,[79] and of their posterity,[80] that they may not be cut off from the privileges of the covenant. Otherwise, if a believer offends, he remains destitute of the remedy provided in that behalf.[81] And should all believers neglect this duty of joining to all particular congregations, it might follow thereupon that Christ should have no visible, political churches upon earth.

CHAPTER V

Of the First Subject of Church Power or, to Whom Church Power Doth First Belong

1. The first subject of church power is either supreme, or subordinate and ministerial. The supreme (by way of gift from the Father) is the Lord Jesus Christ.[82] The ministerial is either extraordinary, as the apostles, prophets, and evangelists;[83] or ordinary;[84] as every particular congregational church.[85]

2. Ordinary church power is either the power of office—that is, such as is proper to the eldership—or power of privilege, such as belongs unto the brotherhood. The latter is in the brethren formally and immediately from Christ—that is, so as it may, according to order, be acted or exercised immediately by themselves;[86] the former is not in them formally or immediately, and therefore cannot be acted or exercised immediately by them,[87] but is said to be in them, in that they design the persons unto office, who only are to act or to exercise this power.[88]

CHAPTER VI

Of the Officers of the Church, and Especially
of Pastors and Teachers

1. A church being a company of people combined together by covenant for the worship of God, it appears thereby, that there may be the essence and being of a church without any officers, seeing there is both the form and matter of a church; which is implied when it is said, "the apostles ordained elders in every church."[89]

2. Nevertheless, though officers not be absolutely necessary to the simple being of churches, when they be called; yet ordinarily to their calling they are, and to their well being;[90] and therefore the Lord Jesus, out of his tender compassion,[91] has appointed and ordained officers,[92] which he would not have done, if they had not been useful and needful for the church; yea, being ascended into heaven, he received gifts for men,[93] and gave gifts to men;[94] whereof officers for the church are justly accounted no small parts, they being to continue to the end of the world, and for the perfecting of all the saints.[95]

3. The officers were either extraordinary or ordinary:[96] extraordinary, as apostles,[97] prophets,[98] evangelists;[99] ordinary, as elders and deacons.[100]

The apostles, prophets, and evangelists, as they were called extraordinarily by Christ,[101] so there office ended with themselves; whence it is that Paul, directing Timothy how to carry along church administrations, gives no direction about the choice or course of apostles, prophets, or evangelists, but only of elders and deacons;[102] and when Paul was to take his last leave of the church of Ephesus, he committed the care of feeding the church to no other, but unto the elders of that church.[103] The like charge does Peter commit to the elders.[104]

4. Of elders (who are also in scripture called bishops)[105] some attend chiefly to the ministry of the word, as the pastors and teachers;[106]

others attend especially unto rule, who are, therefore, called ruling elders.[107]

5. The office of pastor and teacher appears to be distinct. The pastor's special work is to attend to exhortation, and therein to administer a word of wisdom; the teacher is to attend to doctrine, and therein to administer a word of knowledge;[108] and either of them to administer the seals of that covenant, unto the dispensation whereof they are alike called; as also to execute the censures, being but a kind of application of the word: the preaching of which, together with the application thereof, they are alike charged withal.[109]

6. And for as much as both pastors and teachers are given by Christ for the perfecting of the saints and edifying of his body,[110] which saints and body of Christ is his church,[111] therefore we account pastors and teachers to be both of them church officers, and not the pastor for the church, and the teacher only for the schools.[112] Though this we gladly acknowledge: that schools are both lawful, profitable, and necessary for the training up of such in good literature or learning, as may afterwards be called forth unto office of pastor or teacher in the church.[113]

CHAPTER VII

Of Ruling Elders and Deacons

1. The ruling elder's office is distinct from the office of pastor and teacher.[114] The ruling elders are not so called to exclude the pastors and teachers from ruling,[115] but because ruling and governing is common to these with the other; whereas attending to teach and preach the word is peculiar unto the former.[116]

2. The ruling elder's work is to join with the pastor and teacher in those acts of spiritual rule which are distinct from the ministry of the word and sacraments committed to them;[117] of which sort, these be as follows:

    I. To open and shut the doors of God's house: by the admission of members approved by the church,[118] by ordination of officers chosen by the church,[119] and by excommunication of notorious and obstinate offenders renounced by the church,[120] and by restoring of penitents, forgiven by the church.[121]

    II. To call the church together when there is occasion and seasonably to dismiss them again.[122]

    III. To prepare matters in private, that in public they may be carried to an end with less trouble and more speedy dispatch.[123]

    IV. To moderate the carriage of all matters in the church assembled:[124] as, to propound matters to the church, to order the season of speech and silence,[125] and to pronounce sentence according to the mind of Christ with the consent of the church.[126]

    V. To be guides and leaders to the church in all matters whatsoever pertaining to church administrations and actions.

vi. To see that none in the church live inordinately out of rank and place, without a calling, or idly in their calling.

vii. To prevent and heal such offences in life or in doctrine as might corrupt the church.[127]

viii. To feed the flock of God with a word of admonition.[128]

ix. And, as they shall be sent for, to visit and pray over their sick brethren.[129]

x. And at other times, as opportunity shall serve thereunto.[130]

3. The office of a deacon is instituted in the church by the Lord Jesus; sometimes they are called helps.[131] The Scripture tells us how they should be qualified: "grave, not double-tongued, not given to much to wine, not given to filthy lucre."[132] They must first be proved, and then use the office of a deacon, being found blameless.[133] The office and work of a deacon is to receive the offerings of the church, gifts given to the church, and to keep the treasury of the church,[134] and therewith to serve the tables which the church is to provide for: as the Lord's table, the table of the ministers, and of such as are in necessity, to whom they are to distribute in simplicity.[135]

4. The office, therefore, being limited unto the care of the temporal good things of the church,[136] it extends not to the attendance upon and administration of the spiritual things thereof, as the word and sacraments and the like.

5. The ordinance of the Apostle and practice of the church commends the Lord's day as a fit time for the contributions of the saints.[137]

6. The instituting of all these officers in the church is the work of God himself, of the Lord Jesus Christ, of the Holy Ghost.[138] And therefore such officers as he has not appointed are altogether unlawful, either to be placed in the church or to be retained therein, and are to be looked at as human creatures, mere inventions and appointments of man, to the great dishonor of Christ Jesus, the Lord of his house, the King of his church, whether popes, patriarchs, cardinals,

archbishops, lord-bishops, archdeacons, officials, commissaries, and the like. These and the rest of that hierarchy and retinue, not being plants of the Lord's planting, shall all certainly be rooted out and cast forth.[139]

7. The Lord has appointed ancient widows (where they may be had) to minister in the church, in giving attendance to the sick and to give succor unto them and others in the like necessities.[140]

CHAPTER VIII

Of the Election of Church Officers

1. No man may take the honor of a church officer unto himself, but he that was called of God, as was Aaron.[141]

2. Calling unto office is either immediate, by Christ himself—such was the call of the apostles, and prophets;[142] this manner of calling ended with them, as has been said—or mediate, by the church.[143]

3. It is meet that, before any be ordained or chosen officers, they should first be tried and proved, because hands are not suddenly to be laid upon any,[144] and both elders and deacons must be of honest and good report.[145]

4. The things in respect of which they are to be tried are those gifts and virtues which the Scripture requires in men that are to be elected into such places, viz. that elders must be "blameless, sober, apt to teach," and endued with such other qualifications as are laid down.[146] Deacons to be fitted as is directed.[147]

5. Officers are to be called by such churches whereunto they are to minister. Of such moment is the preservation of this power that the churches exercised it in the presence of the apostles.[148]

6. A church, being free, cannot become subject to any but by a free election;[149] yet when such a people do choose any to be over them in the Lord, then do they become subject and most willingly submit to their ministry in the Lord, whom they have so chosen.[150]

7. And if the church have power to choose their officers and ministers, then, in case of manifest unworthiness and delinquency, they have power also to depose them.[151] For to open and shut, to choose and refuse, to constitute in office, and remove from office, are acts belonging unto the same power.

8. We judge it much conducing to the well-being and communion of churches that, where it may conveniently be done, neighbor churches be advised withal and their help made use of in the trial of church officers, in order to their choice.[152]

9. The choice of such church officers belongs not to the civil magistrates as such, or diocesan bishops, or patrons. For of these, or any such like, the Scripture is wholly silent, as having any power therein.

CHAPTER IX

Of Ordination and Imposition of Hands

1. Church officers are not only to be chosen by the church, but also to be ordained by imposition of hands and prayer, with which, at ordination of elders, fasting also is to be joined.[153]

2. This ordination we account nothing else but the solemn putting of a man into his place and office in the church whereunto he had right before by election, being like the installing of a magistrate in the commonwealth.[154]

Ordination therefore is not to go before, but to follow election.[155] The essence and substance of the outward calling of an ordinary officer in the church does not consist in his ordination, but in his voluntary and free election by the church and in his accepting of that election, whereupon is founded the relation between pastor and flock, between such a minister and such a people.

Ordination does not constitute an officer, nor give him the essentials of his office. The apostles were elders, without imposition of hands by men; Paul and Barnabas were officers before that imposition of hands.[156] The posterity of Levi were priests and Levites before hands were laid on them by the children of Israel.

3. In such churches where there are elders, imposition of hands in ordination is to be performed by those elders.[157]

4. In such churches where there are no elders, imposition of hands may be performed by some of the brethren orderly chosen by the church thereunto.[158] For, if the people may elect officers, which is the greater, and wherein the substance of the office consists, they may much more (occasion and need so requiring) impose hands in ordination, which is the less and but the accomplishment of the other.

5. Nevertheless, in such churches where there are no elders, and the church so desire, we see not why imposition of hands may not be

performed by the elders of other churches. Ordinary officers laid hands upon the officers of many churches. The presbytery of Ephesus laid hands upon Timothy an evangelist. The presbytery at Antioch laid hands upon Paul and Barnabas.[159]

6. Church officers are officers to one church, even that particular over which the Holy Ghost has made them overseers.[160] Insomuch as elders are commanded to feed not all flocks, but that flock which is committed to their faith and trust and depends upon them. Nor can constant residence at one congregation be necessary for a minister— no, nor yet lawful—if he be not a minister to one congregation only, but to the church universal; because he may not attend one part only of the church, whereto he is a minister, but he is called to attend unto all the flock.[161]

7. He that is clearly loosed from his office relation unto that church whereof he was a minister cannot be looked at as an officer, nor perform any act of office in any other church, unless he be again orderly called unto office; which, when it shall be, we know nothing to hinder, but imposition of hands also in his ordination ought to be used towards him again. For so Paul the apostle received imposition of hands twice, at least, from Ananias.[162]

CHAPTER X

Of the Power of the Church and Its Presbytery

1. Supreme and lordly power over all the churches upon earth does only belong to Jesus Christ, who is king of the church, and head thereof.[163] He has the government upon his shoulders and has all power given to him, both in heaven and earth.[164]

2. A company of professed believers, ecclesiastically confederate, as they are a church before they have officers and without them; so, even in that estate, subordinate church power under Christ, delegated to them by him, does belong to them, in such a manner as is before expressed, Chapter V, Section 2, and as flowing from the very nature and essence of a church;[165] it being natural to all bodies, and so unto a church body, to be furnished with sufficient power for its own preservation and subsistence.[166]

3. This government of the church is a mixed government (and so has been acknowledged, long before the term "independency" was heard of). In respect of Christ, the head and king of the church, and the sovereign power residing in him and exercised by him, it is a monarchy.[167] In respect of the body, or brotherhood, of the church, and power from Christ granted unto them, it resembles a democracy.[168] In respect of the presbytery and power committed to them, it is an aristocracy.[169]

4. The sovereign power, which is peculiar unto Christ, is exercised:

   I. In calling the church out of the world unto holy fellowship with himself.[170]

   II. In instituting the ordinances of his worship and appointing his ministers and officers for the dispensing of them.[171]

   III. In giving laws for the ordering of all our ways and the ways of his house.[172]

   IV. In giving power and life to all his institutions and to his people by them.[173]

v. In protecting and delivering his church against and from all the enemies of their peace.[174]

5. The power granted by Christ unto the body of the church and brotherhood is a prerogative or privilege which the church doth exercise:

    I. In choosing their own officers, whether elders or deacons.[175]

    II. In admission of their own members. And, therefore, there is great reason they should have power to remove any from their fellowship again. Hence, in case of offense, any one brother has power to convince and admonish an offending brother; and, in case of not hearing him, to take one or two more to set on the admonition; and, in case of not hearing them, to proceed to tell the church; and, as his offense may require, the whole church has power to proceed to the public censure of him, whether by admonition or excommunication;[176] and, upon his repentance, to restore him again unto his former communion.[177]

6. In case an elder offend incorrigibly, the matter so requiring, as the church had power to call him to office,[178] so they have power according to order (the counsel of other churches, where it may be had, directing thereto) to remove him from his office; and, being now but a member, in case he add contumacy to his sin, the church, that had power to receive him into their fellowship, has also the same power to cast him out that they have concerning any other member.[179]

7. Church government, or rule, is placed by Christ in the officers of the church, who are therefore called rulers, while they rule with God. Yet, in case of maladministration, they are subject to the power of the church, according as has been said before. The Holy Ghost frequently—yea, always—where it mentions church rule and church government, ascribes it to elders;[180] whereas the work and duty of the people is expressed in the phrase of "obeying their elders" and "submitting themselves unto them" "in the Lord."[181] So, as it is manifest that an organic or complete church is a body politic, consisting of some that are governors and some that are governed in the Lord.[182]

8. The power which Christ has committed to the elders is to feed and rule the church of God[183] and, accordingly, to call the church together upon any weighty occasion, when the members so called, without just cause, may not refuse to come,[184] nor when they are come, depart before they are dismissed,[185] nor speak in the church before they have leave from the elders, nor continue so doing when they require silence,[186] nor may they oppose nor contradict the judgment or sentence of the elders without sufficient and weighty cause, because such practices are manifestly contrary unto order and government, and inlets of disturbance and tend to confusion.[187]

9. It belongs also unto the elders to examine any officers or members before they be received of the church, to receive the accusations brought to the church, and to prepare them for the church's hearing. In handling of offences and other matters before the church, they have power to declare and publish the counsel and will of God touching the same and to pronounce sentence with the consent of the church.[188] Lastly, they have power, when they dismiss the people, to bless them in the name of the Lord.[189]

10. This power of government in the elders does not any wise prejudice the power of privilege in the brotherhood, as neither the power of privilege in the brethren does prejudice the power of government in the elders; but they may sweetly agree together, as we may see in the example of the apostles, furnished with the greatest church power, who took in the concurrence and consent of the brethren in church administrations.[190] Also that Scripture,[191] does declare that what the churches were to act and do in these matters, they were to do in a way of obedience, and that not only to the direction of the apostles, but also of their ordinary elders.[192]

11. From the premises, namely, that the ordinary power of government belonging only to the elders, power of privilege remains with the brotherhood (as power of judgment in matters of censure and power of liberty in matters of liberty). It follows that, in an organic church and right administration, so as no church act can be consummated or perfected without the consent of both.

CHAPTER XI

Of the Maintenance of Church Officers

1. The Apostle concludes that necessary and sufficient maintenance is due unto the ministers of the word from the law of nature and nations, from the law of Moses, the equity thereof, as also the rule of common reason.[193] Moreover, the Scripture not only calls elders laborers and workmen,[194] but also, speaking of them, says that "the laborer is worthy of his hire"[195] and requires that he which is taught in the word should communicate to him "in all good things"[196] and mentions it, as an ordinance of the Lord, that they which preach the gospel should live of the gospel, and forbids the muzzling of the mouth of the ox that treads out the corn.[197]

2. The Scriptures alleged requiring this maintenance as a bounden duty and due debt, and not as a matter of alms and free gift, therefore people are not at liberty to do or not to do what and when they please in this matter, no more than in any other commanded duty and ordinance of the Lord; but ought of duty to minister of their "carnal things" to them that labor amongst them in the word and doctrine, as well as they ought to pay any other workmen their wages or to discharge and satisfy their other debts or to submit themselves to observe any other ordinance of the Lord.[198]

3. The Apostle, enjoining that he which is taught communicate to him that teaches "in all good things,"[199] does not leave it arbitrary what or how much a man shall give, or in what proportion, but even the latter, as well as the former, is prescribed and appointed by the Lord.[200]

4. Not only members of churches, but "all that are taught in the word," are to contribute unto him that teaches, "in all good things."[201] In case that congregations are defective in their contributions, the deacons are to call upon them to do their duty.[202] If their call suffices not, the church by her power is to require it of their members, and

where church power, through the corruption of men, does not or cannot attain the end, the magistrate is to see ministry duly provided for, as appears from the commended example of Nehemiah.[203] The magistrates are nursing fathers and nursing mothers and stand charged with the custody of both tables;[204] because it is better to prevent a scandal, that it may not come, and easier also, than to remove it when it is given. It is most suitable to rule that, by the church's care, each man should know his proportion according to rule, what he should do before he do it, that so his judgment and heart may be satisfied in what he does and just offense prevented in what is done.[205]

Of Admission of Members into the Church

1. The doors of the churches of Christ upon earth do not by God's appointment stand so wide open that all sorts of people, good or bad, may freely enter therein at their pleasure; but such as are admitted thereto as members ought to be examined and tried first, whether they be fit and meet to be received into church society or not.[206] The eunuch of Ethiopia, before his admission, was examined by Philip, whether he did believe on Jesus Christ with all his heart.[207] The angel of the church at Ephesus is commended for trying such as said they were apostles, and were not.[208] There is like reason for trying of them that profess themselves to be believers.

The officers are charged with the keeping of the doors of the church, and therefore are in a special manner to make trial of the fitness of such who enter. Twelve angels are set at the gates of the temple, lest such as were ceremonially unclean should enter thereinto.[209]

2. The things which are requisite to be found in all church members are repentance from sin and faith in Jesus Christ.[210] And, therefore, these are the things whereof men are to be examined at their admission into the church and which then they must profess and hold forth in such sort as may satisfy rational charity that the things are there indeed. John the Baptist admitted men to baptism, confessing and bewailing their sins;[211] and of others it is said that "they came and confessed, and showed their deeds."[212]

3. The weakest measure of faith is to be accepted in those that desire to be admitted into the church, because weak Christians, if sincere, have the substance of that faith, repentance and holiness, which is required in church members, and such have most need of the ordinances for their confirmation and growth in grace.[213] The Lord Jesus would not quench the smoking flax, nor break the bruised reed, but gather the tender lambs in his arms and carry them gently in his

bosom.[214] Such charity and tenderness is to be used, as the weakest Christian, if sincere, may not be excluded nor discouraged. Severity of examination is to be avoided.

4. In case any, through excessive fear or other infirmity, be unable to make their personal relation of their spiritual estate in public, it is sufficient that the elders, having received private satisfaction, make relation thereof in public before the church, they testifying their assents thereunto; this being the way that tends most to edification. But whereas persons are of better abilities, there it is most expedient that they make their relations and confessions personally with their own mouth, as David professes of himself.[215]

5. A personal and public confession and declaring of God's manner of working upon the soul is both lawful, expedient, and useful in sundry respects and upon sundry grounds. Those three thousand, before they were admitted by the apostles, did manifest that they were pricked in their hearts at Peter's sermon, together with earnest desire to be delivered from their sins, which now wounded their consciences, and their ready receiving of the word of promise and exhortation.[216] We are to be ready to render a reason of the hope that is in us, to every one that asks us;[217] therefore, we must be able and ready upon any occasion to declare and show our repentance for sin, faith unfeigned, and effectual calling, because these are the reason of a well-grounded hope.[218] "I have not hidden your righteousness from the great congregation."[219]

6. This profession of faith and repentance, as it must be made by such at their admission that were never in church society before, so nothing hinders but the same may also be performed by such as have formerly been members of some other church, and the church to which they now join themselves as members may lawfully require the same. Those three thousand,[220] which made their confession, were members of the church of the Jews before; so were they that were baptized by John. Churches may err in their admission and persons regularly admitted may fall into offence. Otherwise, if churches might obtrude their members or if church members might obtrude themselves upon other churches without due trial, the matter so requiring, both the liberty of churches would hereby be infringed, in that they might not examine

those concerning whose fitness for communion they were unsatisfied and, besides the infringing of their liberty, the churches themselves would unavoidably be corrupted and the ordinances defiled;[221] while they might not refuse, but must receive the unworthy, which is contrary unto the Scripture teaching that all churches are sisters and therefore equal.[222]

7. The like trial is to be required from such members of the church as were born in the same or received their membership and were baptized in their infancy or minority by virtue of the covenant of their parents, when being grown up unto years of discretion, they shall desire to be made partakers of the Lord's Supper, unto which, because holy things must not be given unto the unworthy,[223] therefore it is requisite that these, as well as others, should come to their trial and examination and manifest their faith and repentance, by an open profession thereof, before they are received to the Lord's Supper and, otherwise, not to be admitted thereunto.

Yet these church members that were so born or received in their childhood, before they are capable of being made partakers of full communion, have many privileges which others (not church members) have not: they are in covenant with God, have the seal thereof upon them, viz. baptism, and so, if not regenerated, yet are in a more hopeful way of attaining regenerating grace and all the spiritual blessings, both of the covenant and seal; they are also under church watch and, consequently, subject to the reprehensions, admonitions, and censures thereof, for their healing and amendment, as need shall require.

CHAPTER XIII

Of Church Members, Their Removal from One Church to Another, and of Letters of Recommendation and Dismission

1. Church members may not remove or depart from the church, and so one from another as they please, nor without just and weighty cause, but ought to live and dwell together, forasmuch as they are commanded not to forsake the assembling of themselves together.[224] Such departure tends to the dissolution and ruin of the body, as the pulling of stones and pieces of timber from the building, and of members from the natural body, tend to the destruction of the whole.

2. It is, therefore, the duty of church members, in such times and places when counsel may be had, to consult with the church whereof they are members about their removal, that, accordingly, they have their approbation, may be encouraged, or otherwise desist.[225] They who are joined with consent should not depart without consent, except forced thereunto.

3. If a member's departure be manifestly unsafe and sinful, the church may not consent thereunto; for in so doing they should not act in faith and should partake with him in his sin.[226] If the case be doubtful and the person not to be persuaded, it seems best to leave the matter unto God and not forcibly to detain him.[227]

4. Just reasons for a member's removal of himself from the church are:

    I. If a man cannot continue without partaking in sin.[228]

    II. In case of personal persecution: so Paul departed from the disciples at Damascus. Also, in case of general persecution, when all are scattered.[229]

iii. In case of real, and not only pretended, want of competent subsistence, a door being opened for a better supply in another place, together with the means of spiritual edification.[230]

In these, or like cases, a member may lawfully remove and the church cannot lawfully detain him.

5. To separate from a church, either out of contempt of their holy fellowship; or out of covetousness, or for greater enlargements, with just grief to the church;[231] or out of schism, or want of love;[232] and out of a spirit of contention in respect of some unkindness,[233] or some evil only conceived, or indeed, in the church, which might and should be tolerated and healed with a spirit of meekness,[234] and of which evil the church is not yet convinced (though perhaps himself be) nor admonished; for these or the like reasons to withdraw from public communion, in word or seals or censures, is unlawful and sinful.

6. Such members as have orderly removed their habitation ought to join themselves unto the church in order where they do inhabit, if it may be;[235] otherwise they can neither perform the duties nor receive the privileges of members.[236] Such an example, tolerated in some, is apt to corrupt others; which, if many should follow, would threaten the dissolution and confusion of churches, contrary to the Scripture.[237]

7. Order requires that a member, thus removing, have letters testimonial and of dismission from the church, whereof he yet is, unto the church whereunto he desires to be joined,[238] lest the church should be deluded; that the church may receive him in faith and not be corrupted by receiving deceivers and false brethren. Until the person dismissed be received into another church, he ceases not by his letters of dismission to be a member of the church whereof he was. The church cannot make a member no member but by excommunication.

8. If a member be called to remove only for a time where a church is, letters of recommendation are requisite and sufficient for communion with that church, in the ordinances, and in their watch; as Phoebe, a servant of the church at Cenchrea, had letters written for her to the church of Rome, that she might be received as becomes saints.[239]

9. Such letters of recommendation and dismission were written for Apollos,[240] for Marcus to the Colossians,[241] for Phoebe to the Romans,[242] for sundry others to other churches. And the Apostle tells us that some persons, not sufficiently known otherwise, have special need of such letters, though he, for his part, had no need thereof.[243] The use of them is to be a benefit and help to the party for whom they are written, and for the furthering of his receiving amongst the saints in the place whereto he goes; and the due satisfaction of them in their receiving of him.

CHAPTER XIV

Of Excommunication and Other Censures

1. The censures of the church are appointed by Christ for the preventing, removing, and healing of offenses in the church; for the reclaiming and gaining of offending brethren; for the deterring others from the like offenses;[244] for purging out the leaven which may infect the whole lump;[245] for vindicating the honor of Christ and of his church and the holy profession of the gospel; and for preventing the wrath of God that may justly fall upon the church if they should suffer his covenant and the seals thereof to be profaned by notorious and obstinate offenders.[246]

2. If an offense be private (one brother offending another), the offender is to go and acknowledge his repentance for it unto his offended brother, who is then to forgive him.[247] But if the offender neglect or refuse to do it, the brother offended is to go and convince and admonish him of it, between themselves privately. If, thereupon, the offender be brought to repent of his offense, the admonisher has won his brother, but if the offender hear not his brother, the brother offended is to take with him one or two more that, in the mouth of two or three witnesses, every word may be established (whether the word of admonition, if the offender receive it, or the word of complaint, if he refuse it); for if he refuse it, the offended brother is by the mouth of elders to tell the church and if he hear the church and declare the same by penitent confession, he is recovered and gained; and if the church discern him to be willing to hear, yet not fully convinced of his offense, as in case of heresy, they are to dispense to him a public admonition, which, declaring the offender to lie under the public offence of the church, does thereby withhold or suspend him from the holy fellowship of the Lord's Supper till his offense be removed by penitent confession. If he still continue obstinate, they are to cast him out by excommunication.[248]

3. But if the offense be more public at first, and of a more heinous and criminal nature, to wit, such as are condemned by the light of nature, then the church, without such gradual proceeding, is to cast out the offender from their holy communion for the further mortifying of his sin and the healing of his soul in the day of the Lord Jesus.[249]

4. In dealing with an offender, great care is to be taken that we be neither over strict or rigorous, nor too indulgent or remiss. Our proceeding herein ought to be with a spirit of meekness, considering ourselves, lest we also be tempted, and that the best of us have need of much forgiveness from the Lord.[250] Yet, the winning and healing of the offender's soul being the end of these endeavors, we must not daub with untempered mortar nor heal the wounds of our brethren slightly.[251] On some, have compassion; others, save with fear.

5. While the offender remains excommunicate, the church is to refrain from all member-like communion with him in spiritual things and also from all familiar communion with him in civil things, farther than the necessity of natural or domestical or civil relations do require; and are therefore to forbear to eat and drink with him, that he may be ashamed.[252]

6. Excommunication, being a spiritual punishment, it does not prejudice the excommunicate in, nor deprive him of, his civil rights and therefore touches not princes or other magistrates in point of their civil dignity or authority. And, the excommunicate being but as a publican and a heathen, heathens being lawfully permitted to come to hear the word in church assemblies,[253] we acknowledge therefore the like liberty of hearing the word may be permitted to persons excommunicate that is permitted unto heathen.[254] And, because we are not without hope of his recovery, we are not to account him as an enemy, but to admonish him as a brother.

7. If the Lord sanctify the censure to the offender, so, as by the grace of Christ, he does testify his repentance with humble confession of his sin and judging of himself, giving glory unto God, the church is then to forgive him and to comfort him and to restore him to the wonted brotherly communion which formerly he enjoyed with them.[255]

8. The suffering of profane or scandalous livers to continue in fellowship and partake in the sacraments is doubtless a great sin in those that have power in their hands to redress it and do it not.[256] Nevertheless, inasmuch as Christ and his apostles, in their times, and the prophets and other godly in theirs, did lawfully partake of the Lord's commanded ordinances in the Jewish church and neither taught nor practiced separation from the same, though unworthy ones were permitted therein,[257] and inasmuch as the faithful in the church of Corinth, wherein were many unworthy persons and practices, are never commanded to absent themselves from the sacraments because of the same, therefore the godly, in like cases, are not presently to separate.[258]

9. As separation from such a church wherein profane and scandalous livers are tolerated is not presently necessary, so, for the members thereof, otherwise worthy, hereupon to abstain from communicating with such a church in the participation of the sacraments is unlawful.[259] For as it were unreasonable for an innocent person to be punished for the faults of others, wherein he has no hand and whereunto he gave no consent,[260] so it is more unreasonable that a godly man should neglect duty and punish himself in not coming for his portion in the blessing of the seals, as he ought, because others are suffered to come that ought not, especially considering that himself does neither consent to their sin nor to their approaching to the ordinance in their sin nor to the neglect of others, who should put them away and do not, but, on the contrary, does heartily mourn for these things, and does modestly and seasonably stir up others to do their duty.[261] If the church cannot be reformed, they may use their liberty, as is specified, Chapter 13:4. But this all the godly are bound unto, even every one to do his endeavor, according to his power and place, that the unworthy may be duly proceeded against by the church, to whom this matter does appertain.

CHAPTER XV

Of the Communion of Churches One with Another

1. Although churches be distinct, and therefore may not be confounded one with another, and equal, and therefore have not dominion one over another, yet all the churches ought to preserve church communion one with another, because they are all united unto Christ, not only as a mystical, but as a political head; whence is derived a communion suitable thereunto.[262]

2. The communion of churches is exercised sundry ways.

    I. By way of mutual care in taking thought for one another's welfare.[263]

    II. By way of consultation one with another, when we have occasion to require the judgment and counsel of other churches touching any person or cause wherewith they may be better acquainted than ourselves. As the church of Antioch consulted with the apostles and elders of the church at Jerusalem about the question of circumcision of the gentiles and about the false teachers that broached that doctrine.[264] In which case, when any church wants light or peace amongst themselves, it is a way of communion of churches, according to the word, to meet together by their elders and other messengers in a synod to consider and argue the points in doubt or difference and, having found out the way of truth and peace, to commend the same by their letters and messengers to the churches whom the same may concern.[265] But if a church be rent with divisions amongst themselves or lie under any open scandal, and yet refuse to consult with other churches for healing or removing of the same, it is matter of just offense both to the Lord Jesus and to other churches, as betraying too much want of mercy and faithfulness, not to seek to bind up the breaches and wounds of the church and brethren.[266] And, therefore, the state of such a church calls aloud upon other churches to exercise a fuller act of brotherly communion, to wit, by way of admonition.

III. A third way, then, of communion of churches is by way of admonition, to wit, in case any public offense be found in a church, which they either discern not or are slow in proceeding to use the means for the removing and healing of. Paul had no authority over Peter, yet when he saw Peter not walking with a right foot, he publicly rebuked him before the church.[267] Though churches have no more authority one over another than one apostle had over another; yet as one apostle might admonish another, so may one church admonish another, and yet without usurpation. In which case, if the church that lies under offense does not hearken to the church which does admonish her, the church is to acquaint other neighbor churches with that offense, which the offending church still lies under, together with their neglect of the brotherly admonition given unto them. Whereupon those other churches are to join in seconding the admonition formerly given and, if still the offending church continue in obstinacy and impenitence, they may forbear communion with them and are to proceed to make use of the help of a synod or counsel of neighbor churches walking orderly, if a greater cannot conveniently be had, for their conviction. If they hear not the synod, the synod having declared them to be obstinate, particular churches, approving and accepting of the judgment of the synod, are to declare the sentence of non-communion respectively concerning them and thereupon, out of a religious care to keep their own communion pure, they may justly withdraw themselves from participation with them at the Lord's Table and from such other acts of holy communion as the communion of churches does otherwise allow and require.[268] Nevertheless, if any members of such a church as lies under public offense do not consent to the offense of the church, but do in due sort bear witness against it, they are still to be received to wonted communion;

for it is not equal that the innocent should suffer with the offensive.[269] Yea, furthermore, if such innocent members, after due waiting in the use of all good means for the healing of the offense of their own church, shall at last, with the allowance of the counsel of neighbor churches, withdraw from the fellowship of their own church and offer themselves to the fellowship of another, we judge it lawful for the other church to receive them, being otherwise fit, as if they had been orderly dismissed to them from their own church.

IV. A fourth way of communion of churches is by way of participation. The members of one church occasionally coming unto another, we willingly admit them to partake with us at the Lord's Table, it being the seal of our communion not only with Christ, nor only with the members of our own church, but also with all the churches of the saints;[270] in which regard we refuse not to baptize their children presented to us, if either their own minister be absent or such a fruit of holy fellowship be desired with us. In like case such churches as are furnished with more ministers than one do willingly afford one of their own ministers to supply the place of an absent or sick minister of another church for a needful season.

V. A fifth way of church communion is by way of recommendation, when a member of one church has occasion to reside in another church.[271] If but for a season, we commend him to their watchful fellowship by letters of recommendation, but, if he be called to settle his abode there, we commit him according to his desire to the fellowship of their covenant by letters of dismission.[272]

VI. A sixth way of church communion is, in case of need, to minister relief and succor one unto another: either of able members to furnish them with officers or of outward support to the necessities of poorer churches, as did the churches of the gentiles contribute liberally to the poor saints at Jerusalem.[273]

49

3. When a company of believers purpose to gather into church fellowship, it is requisite for their safer proceeding and the maintaining of the communion of churches that they signify their intent unto the neighbor churches, walking according to the order of the gospel, and desire their presence and help and right hand of fellowship, which they ought readily to give unto them when there is no just cause of excepting against their proceedings.[274]

4. Besides these several ways of communion, there is also a way of propagation of churches. When a church shall grow too numerous, it is a way, and fit season, to propagate one church out of another by sending forth such of their members as are willing to remove and to procure some officers to them, as may enter with them into church estate amongst themselves.[275] As bees, when the hive is too full, issue forth by swarms and are gathered into other hives, so the churches of Christ may do the same upon like necessity and therein hold forth to them the right hand of fellowship, both in their gathering into a church and in the ordination of their officers.

CHAPTER XVI

Of Synods

1. Synods, orderly assembled, and rightly proceeding according to the pattern, Acts 15, we acknowledge as the ordinance of Christ;[276] and though not absolutely necessary to the being, yet many times, through the iniquity of men and perverseness of times, necessary to the well-being of churches for the establishment of truth and peace therein.

2. Synods, being spiritual and ecclesiastical assemblies, are therefore made up of spiritual and ecclesiastical causes. The next efficient cause of them, under Christ, is the power of the churches sending forth their elders and other messengers,[277] who, being met together in the name of Christ, are the matter of a synod;[278] and they in arguing, debating, and determining matters of religion according to the word,[279] and publishing the same to the churches whom it concerns,[280] do put forth the proper and formal acts of a synod, to the conviction of errors, and heresies, and the establishment of truth and peace in the churches, which is the end of a synod.[281]

3. Magistrates have power to call a synod, by calling to the churches to send forth their elders and other messengers to counsel and assist them in matters of religion;[282] but yet the constituting of a synod is a church act and may be transacted by the churches, even when civil magistrates may be enemies to churches and to church assemblies.[283]

4. It belongs to synods and councils to debate and determine controversies of faith and cases of conscience;[284] to clear from the word holy directions for the holy worship of God and good government of the church;[285] to bear witness against maladministration and corruption in doctrine or manners in any particular church and to give directions for the reformation thereof;[286] not to exercise church censures in way of discipline, nor any other act of church authority or jurisdiction which that presidential synod did forbear.

5. The synod's directions and determinations, so far as consonant to the word of God, are to be received with reverence and submission, not only for their agreement therewith (which is the principal ground thereof and without which they bind not at all), but also, secondarily, for the power whereby they are made, as being an ordinance of God appointed thereunto in his word.[287]

6. Because it is difficult, if not impossible, for many churches to come altogether in one place, in all their members universally; therefore they may assemble by their delegates or messengers, as the church of Antioch went not all to Jerusalem, but some select men for that purpose.[288] Because none are, or should be, more fit to know the state of the churches nor to advise of ways for the good thereof than elders, therefore it is fit that, in the choice of the messengers for such assemblies, they have special respect unto such.[289] Yet inasmuch as not only Paul and Barnabas, but certain others also, were sent to Jerusalem from Antioch,[290] and when they were come to Jerusalem, not only the apostles and elders, but other brethren also, do assemble and meet about the matter, therefore synods are to consist both of elders and other church members, endued with gifts and sent by the churches, not excluding the presence of any brethren in the churches.

CHAPTER XVII

Of the Civil Magistrate's Power
in Matters Ecclesiastical

1. It is lawful, profitable, and necessary for Christians to gather themselves into church estate and therein to exercise all the ordinances of Christ according unto the word,[291] although the consent of magistrate could not be had thereunto, because the apostles and Christians in their time did frequently thus practice, when the magistrates being all of them Jewish or pagan, and mostly persecuting enemies, would give no countenance or consent to such matters.[292]

2. Church government stands in no opposition to civil government of commonwealths, nor any intrenches upon the authority of civil magistrates in their jurisdictions, nor any whit weakens their hands in governing,[293] but rather strengthens them and furthers the people in yielding more hearty and conscionable obedience unto them, whatsoever some ill-affected persons to the ways of Christ have suggested to alienate the affections of kings and princes from the ordinances of Christ; as if the kingdom of Christ in his church could not rise and stand without the falling and weakening of their government, which is also of Christ. Whereas the contrary is more true, that they may both stand together and flourish, the one being helpful unto the other in their distinct and due administrations.[294]

3. The power and authority of magistrates is not for the restraining of churches or any other good works, but for helping in and furthering thereof. And, therefore, the consent and countenance of magistrates, when it may be had, is not to be slighted or lightly esteemed, but, on the contrary; it is part of that honor due to Christian magistrates to desire and crave their consent and approbation therein; which being obtained, the churches may then proceed in their way with much more encouragement and comfort.[295]

4. It is not in the power of magistrates to compel their subjects to become church members and to partake at the Lord's Table; for the priests are reproved that brought unworthy ones into the sanctuary.[296] Then, as it was unlawful for the priests, so it is as unlawful to be done by civil magistrates. Those whom the church is to cast out if they were in, the magistrate ought not to thrust into the church nor to hold them therein.[297]

5. As it is unlawful for church officers to meddle with the sword of the magistrate, so it is unlawful for the magistrate to meddle with the work proper to church officers.[298] The acts of Moses and David, who were not only princes but prophets, were extraordinary, therefore, not imitable. Against such usurpation the Lord witnessed by smiting Uzziah with leprosy for presuming to offer incense.[299]

6. It is the duty of the magistrate to take care of matters of religion and to improve his civil authority for the observing of the duties commanded in the first, as well as for observing of the duties commanded in the second table. They are called gods.[300] The end of the magistrate's office is not only the "quiet and peaceable life" of the subject, in matters of righteousness and honesty, but also in matters of godliness—yea, of all godliness.[301] Moses, Joshua, David, Solomon, Asa, Jehoshaphat, Hezekiah, Josiah, are much commended by the Holy Ghost for the putting forth their authority in matters of religion.[302] On the contrary, such kings as have been failing this way are frequently taxed and reproved by the Lord.[303] And not only the kings of Judah, but also Job, Nehemiah, the king of Nineveh, Darius, Artaxerxes, Nebuchadnezzar, whom none looked at as types of Christ (though were it so, there were no place for any just objection), are commended in the book of God for exercising their authority this way.[304]

7. The objects of the power of the magistrate are not things merely inward, and so not subject to his cognizance and view, as unbelief, hardness of heart, erroneous opinions not vented, but only such things as are acted by the outward man. Neither is their power to be exercised in commanding such acts of the outward man and punishing the neglect thereof, as are but mere inventions, and devices of men,[305] but about such acts as are commanded and forbidden in the word—yea,

such as the word does clearly determine, though not always clearly to the judgment of the magistrate or others, yet clearly in itself. In these he of right ought to put forth his authority, though oft times actually he does it not.[306]

8. Idolatry, blasphemy, heresy, venting corrupt and pernicious opinions that destroy the foundation, open contempt of the word preached, profanation of the Lord's Day, disturbing the peaceable administration and exercise of the worship and holy things of God, and the like are to be restrained and punished by civil authority.[307]

9. If any church, one or more, shall grow schismatical, rending itself from the communion of other churches, or shall walk incorrigibly or obstinately in any corrupt way of their own, contrary to the rule of the word, in such case the magistrate is to put forth his coercive power, as the matter shall require. The tribes on this side Jordan intended to make war against the other tribes for building the altar of witness, whom they suspected to have turned away therein from following of the Lord.[308]

SCRIPTURE REFERENCES

1. Galatians 2.15; Acts 26.6–7
2. Acts 11.20–21
3. Galatians 2.14
4. William Ames, *De Conscientia* (1635)
5. Song of Solomon 8.8–9
6. Song of Solomon 4.12–13
7. John 3.25–30
8. Philippians 3.15–16; Ephesians 4.3
9. Ezekiel 43.10–11
10. Exodus 10.7
11. John 17.20–23
12. John 11.42
13. Ezra 4.1–3
14. 2 John 10.11
15. Ezekiel 43.11; Colossians 2.5; 1 Timothy 3.15
16. Hebrews 3.5–6
17. Exodus 25.40
18. 2 Timothy 3.16
19. 1 Chronicles 15.13; Exodus 20.4
20. 1 Timothy 3.15, 6.13, 16
21. Hebrews 12.27–28
22. 1 Corinthians 15.24
23. Deuteronomy 12.32; Ezekiel 43.8; 1 Kings 12.31–33
24. 1 Kings 12.28–29; Isaiah 28.13; Colossians 2.22–23; Acts 15.28
25. Matthew 15.9; 1 Corinthians 11.23
26. 1 Corinthians 7.35, 14.26, 40
27. 1 Corinthians 11.14, 16
28. 1 Corinthians 14.12, 19
29. Acts 15.28
30. Ephesians 1.22, 5.25–26, 30; Hebrews 12.23
31. Romans 8.17; 2 Timothy 2.12, 4.8
32. Ephesians 6.12–13
33. 2 Timothy 2.19; Revelation 2.17; 1 Corinthians 6.17
34. Romans 1.8; 1 Thessalonians 1.8; Isaiah 2.2; 1 Timothy 6.12
35. Acts 19.1
36. Colossians 2.5
37. Matthew 18.17; 1 Corinthians 5.12
38. Genesis 18.19
39. Exodus 19.6
40. 1 Corinthians 14.23, 36
41. 1 Corinthians 1.2
42. Exodus 19.5–6; Deuteronomy 29.1, 9–15
43. Acts 2.42
44. 1 Corinthians 12.27, 14.26
45. 1 Corinthians 1.2; Ephesians 1.1
46. Hebrews 6.1, 1 Corinthians 1.5, Romans 15.14
47. Psalms 50.16–17
48. Acts 8.37; Matthew 3.6 (Acts 8.37 is a controversial passage often left out of modern Bibles because it is not found in the oldest extant Greek manuscripts. It says, "And Philip said, 'If you believe with all your heart, you may.' And he replied, 'I believe that Jesus Christ is the Son of God.'")
49. Romans 6.17
50. 1 Corinthians 1.2; Philippians 1.1; Colossians 1.2; Ephesians 1.1
51. 1 Corinthians 5.2, 13
52. Revelation 2.14–15; Ezekiel 23.38–39, 44.7–9
53. Numbers 19.20; Haggai 2.13–14; 1 Corinthians 11.27–29; Psalms 37.21
54. 1 Corinthians 5.6
55. 1 Corinthians 7.14
56. Jeremiah 2.21
57. 1 Corinthians 5.12; Galatians 5.4

58. Jeremiah 14; 2 Corinthians 12.21; Revelation 2
59. 1 Corinthians 14.21; Matthew 18.17
60. Romans 16.1; 1 Thessalonians 1.1; Revelation 2.8, 3.7
61. 1 Corinthians 16.1, 19; Galatians 1.2; 2 Corinthians 8.1; 1 Thessalonians 2.14
62. Acts 2.46, 5.12, 6.2, 14.27, 15.38, 1 Corinthians 5.4, 14.23
63. Romans 16.1
64. Acts 20.28
65. 1 Corinthians 12.27; 1 Timothy 3.15
66. 1 Corinthians 12.15–17
67. Ephesians 2.19–22
68. Revelations 2
69. Exodus 19.5, 8; Deuteronomy 29.12–13
70. Zechariah 9.11; 11.14
71. Ephesians 2.19; 2 Corinthians 11.2
72. Genesis 17.7; Deuteronomy 29.12–13
73. Ephesians 2.12, 19
74. Exodus 19.5–8; 24.3, 17; Joshua 24.18–24
75. Psalms 50.5; Nehemiah 9.38, 10.1; Genesis 17; Deuteronomy 29
76. Acts 2.47, 9.26; Matthew 3.13–15, 28.19–20; Psalms 133.2–3, 87.7
77. Matthew 18.20; 1 John 1.3
78. Psalms 119.176; 1 Peter 2.25
79. Ephesians 4.16
80. John 21.24–25
81. Matthew 18.15–17
82. Matthew 28.18; Revelations 3.7; Isaiah 9.6
83. John 20.21–23
84. 1 Corinthians 14.32
85. Titus 1.5; 1 Corinthians 5.12
86. Romans 12.4–8
87. 1 Corinthians 12.29–30
88. Acts 1.23; 6.3–4; 14.23
89. Acts 14.23
90. Romans 10.17
91. Jeremiah 3.15

92. 1 Corinthians 12.28; Ephesians 4.11
93. Psalms 68.18
94. Ephesians 4.8
95. Ephesians 4.11–13
96. 1 Corinthians 12.28; Ephesians 4.11
97. Galatians 1.1; Acts 8.16–19
98. Acts 11.28
99. Acts 8.6
100. Romans 11.7–8
101. 1 Corinthians 4.9
102. 1 Timothy 3.1–2; 8–13; Titus 1.5
103. Acts 20.17, 28
104. 1 Peter 5.1–3
105. 1 Timothy 3.2; Philippians 1.1; Acts 20.17, 28; 1 Timothy 5.17
106. Ephesians 4.11
107. Romans 12.7–8
108. 1 Corinthians 12.8
109. 2 Timothy 4.1–2; Titus 1.9
110. Ephesians 4.11–12
111. Ephesians 1.22–23
112. 1 Samuel 10.12, 19–20
113. 2 Kings 2.3, 15
114. Romans 12.7–9
115. 1 Timothy 5.17
116. 1 Corinthians 12.28; Hebrews 13.17
117. 1 Timothy 5.17
118. 2 Chronicles 23.19; Revelation 21.12
119. 1 Timothy 4.14
120. Matthew 18.17
121. 2 Corinthians 2.7–8
122. Acts 2.6
123. Acts 21.18, 22–23
124. Acts 6.2–3
125. Acts 13.15
126. 2 Corinthians 8.10; Hebrews 13.7, 17, 2; Thessalonians 2.10–12
127. Acts 20.28–32
128. 1 Thessalonians 5:12
129. James 5.14
130. Acts 20.20
131. Acts 6.3, 6; Philippians 1.1.1; Corinthians 12.28
132. 1 Timothy 3.8

133. 1 Timothy 3.9
134. Acts 4.35
135. Acts 6.2–3; Romans 12.8
136. 1 Corinthians 7.17
137. 1 Corinthians 16.1–3
138. 1 Corinthians 12.28; Ephesians 4.8,
    11; Acts 20.28
139. Matthew 15.13
140. 1 Timothy 5.9–10
141. Hebrews 5.4
142. Galatians 1.1
143. Acts 14.23, 6.3
144. 1 Timothy 5.22
145. 1 Timothy 5.7, 10; Acts 16.2, 6.3
146. 1 Timothy 3.2; Titus 1.6–9
147. Acts 6.3; 1 Timothy 3.8–11
148. Acts 14.23, 1.23, 6.3–5
149. Galatians 5.13
150. Hebrews 13.17
151. Romans 16.17
152. Song of Solomon 8.8–9
153. Acts 13.3, 14.23; 1 Timothy 5.22
154. Numbers 8.10; Acts 6.5–6, 13.2–3
155. Acts 6.5–6, 14.23
156. Acts 13.3
157. 1 Timothy 4.14; Acts 13.3;
    1 Timothy 5.22
158. Numbers 8.10
159. 1 Timothy 4.14; Acts 13.3
160. 1 Peter 5.2
161. Acts 20.28
162. Acts 9.17, 13.3
163. Psalms 2.6; Ephesians 1.21–22
164. Isaiah 9.6; Matthew 28.18
165. Acts 1.23, 14.23, 6.3–4
166. Matthew 18.17; 1 Corinthians 5.4–5
167. Revelation 3.7
168. 1 Corinthians 5.12
169. 1 Timothy 5.17
170. Galatians 1.4; Revelations 5.8–9
171. Matthew 28.20; Ephesians 4.8, 11
172. James 4.12; Isaiah 33.22; 1 Timothy
    3.15
173. 2 Corinthians 10.4–5; Isaiah 32.2
174. Luke 1.71
175. Acts 6.3, 5, 14.23, 9.26
176. Matthew 18.15–17; Titus 3.10
177. Colossians 4.17; 2 Corinthians 2.7–8
178. Colossians 4.17
179. Romans 16.17; Matthew 18.17
180. 1 Timothy 5.17; Hebrews 13.7
181. Hebrews 13.17; 1 Thessalonians 5.12
182. Romans 12.8; 1 Corinthians
    12.28–29
183. Acts 20.28; Acts 6.2
184. Numbers 16.12
185. Ezekiel 46.10
186. Acts 13.15
187. Hosea 4.4
188. Revelation 2.2; 1 Timothy 5.19;
    Acts 21.18, 22–23; 1 Corinthians
    5.4–5
189. Numbers 6.23–26
190. Acts 14.15, 23, 6.2; 1 Corinthians
    5.4; 2 Corinthians 2.6–7
191. 2 Corinthians 2.9, 10.6
192. Hebrews 13.17
193. 1 Corinthians 9.9, 14–15
194. Matthew 9.38
195. Matthew 10.10; 1 Timothy 5.18
196. Galatians 6.6
197. 1 Corinthians 9.9; 1 Timothy 5.18
198. Romans 15.27; 1 Corinthians 9.14
199. Galatians 6.6
200. 1 Corinthians 16.2
201. Galatians 6.6
202. Acts 6.3–4
203. Nehemiah 13.11
204. Isaiah 49.23
205. 2 Corinthians 8.12–14
206. Matthew 13.25; Matthew 22.12
207. Acts 8.37 (many modern transla-
    tions of the Bible omit this verse)
208. Revelation 2.2; Acts 9.26
209. 2 Chronicles 23.19; Revelation 21.12
210. Acts 2.38–42; 8.37
211. Matthew 3.6
212. Acts 19.18

213. Romans 14.1
214. Matthew 12.20; Isaiah 40.11
215. Psalms 66.16
216. Acts 2.37, 41
217. 1 Peter 3.15
218. Hebrews 11.1; Ephesians 1.18
219. Psalms 40.10
220. Acts 2
221. Matthew 3.5–6; Galatians 2.4;
     1 Timothy 5.24
222. Song of Solomon 8.8
223. Matthew 7.6; 1 Corinthians 11.27
224. Hebrews 10.25
225. Proverbs 11.16
226. Romans 14.23; 1 Timothy 5.22
227. Acts 21.14
228. Ephesians 5.11
229. Acts 9.25, 29–30, 8.1
230. Nehemiah 13.20
231. 2 Timothy 4.10
232. Romans 16.17
233. Jude 19
234. Ephesians 4.2–3; Colossians 3.13;
     Galatians 6.1–2
235. Isaiah 56.8
236. Acts 9.26
237. 1 Corinthians 14.33
238. Acts 18.27
239. Romans 16.1–2; 2 Corinthians 3.1
240. Acts 18.27
241. Colossians 4.10
242. Romans 16.1–2
243. 2 Corinthians 3.1
244. 1 Timothy 5.20; Deuteronomy
     17.12–13; Jude 22–23; Deuteronomy
     13.11
245. 1 Corinthians 5.6
246. Romans 2.24; Revelation
     2.14–16, 20
247. Matthew 5.23–24; Luke 17.3–4
248. Matthew 18.15–17; Titus 3.10
249. 1 Corinthians 5.4–5, 11
250. Galatians 6.1; Matthew 18.34–35;
     Matthew 6.14–15

251. Ezekiel 13.10; Jeremiah 6.14
252. Matthew 18.17; 1 Corinthians 5.11;
     2 Thessalonians 3.6, 14
253. 1 Corinthians 14.24–25
254. 2 Thessalonians 3.14
255. 2 Corinthians 2.7–8
256. Revelation 2.14–15, 20
257. Matthew 23.3; Acts 3.1
258. 1 Corinthians 6, 15.12
259. 2 Chronicles 30.18
260. Genesis 18.25
261. Ezekiel 9.4
262. Revelation 1.4; Song of Solomon
     8.8; Romans 16.16; 1 Corinthians
     16.19; Acts 15.23; Revelation 2.1
263. Song of Solomon 8.8
264. Acts 15.2
265. Acts 15.6, 22–23
266. Ezekiel 34.4
267. Galatians 2.11–14
268. Matthew 18.15–17 (The writers of
     the Platform believed that the same
     principles should apply to churches
     as to people.)
269. Genesis 18.25
270. 1 Corinthians 12.13
271. Romans 16.1
272. Acts 18.27
273. Acts 11.22, 29; Romans 15.26–27
274. Galatians 2.1–2, 9 (see comment in
     note 268)
275. Isaiah 40.20; Song of Songs 8.8–9
276. Acts 15.2–35
277. Acts 15.2–3
278. Acts 15.6
279. Acts 15.7–21
280. Acts 15.22–23
281. Acts 15.31, 16.4, 15
282. 2 Chronicles 29.4–11
283. Acts 15
284. Acts 15.1–2, 6–7; 1 Chronicles 15.13
285. Acts 15.24, 28–29
286. 2 Chronicles 29.6–7
287. Acts 15

288. Acts 15.2
289. Acts 15.2, 22–23
290. Acts 15
291. Acts 2.41–47
292. Acts 4.1–3
293. John 18.36; Acts 25.8
294. Isaiah 49.23
295. Romans 13.4; 1 Timothy 2.2
296. Ezekiel 44.7–9
297. 1 Corinthians 5.11
298. Matthew 20.25–26
299. 2 Chronicles 26.16–19
300. Psalms 82.1–2

301. 1 Timothy 2.1–2
302. 1 Kings 15.14, 22.43; 2 Kings 12.3, 14.4, 15.35
303. 1 Kings 20.42
304. Job 29.25, 31.26–28; Nehemiah 13, Jonah 3.7–8; Ezra 7; Daniel 3.29
305. 1 Kings 20.28
306. 1 Kings 20.42
307. Deuteronomy 13; 1 Kings 20.28, 42; Daniel 3.29; Zechariah 13.3; Nehemiah 13.21; 1 Timothy 2.2; Romans 13.4
308. Joshua 22

BIBLIOGRAPHY

PRINTED VERSIONS OF THE PLATFORM

The Cambridge Platform of Church Discipline. Boston: Perkins and Whipple, 1850.

Davis, Robert E. *Historic Documents of Congregationalism.* Boston: Puritan Press, 2005.

Walker, Williston. *The Creeds and Platforms of Congregationalism.* Boston: Pilgrim Press, 1960.

WORKS CONTEMPORARY WITH THE PLATFORM

Cotton, John. *The Way of the Congregational Churches Cleared.* London: printed by M. Simmons for J. Bellamie, 1648.

Hooker, Thomas. *Survey of the Summe of Church Discipline.* London: printed by A.M. for J. Bellamie, 1648.

CELEBRATIONS OF THE PLATFORM

Bulletin of the Congregational Library, vol. 49/50 (Spring/Summer/Fall 1998). A commemorative issue on the Cambridge Platform.

Foote, Henry Wilder, ed. *The Cambridge Platform of 1648, Tercentenary Commemoration at Cambridge, Massachusetts, October 27, 1948.* Boston: Beacon Press and Pilgrim Press, 1949.

OTHER SECONDARY WORKS

Atkins, Gaius Green, and Fagley, Frederick L. *History of American Congregationalism.* Boston and Chicago: Pilgrim Press, 1942.

Cooper, James F. *Tenacious of Their Liberties: The Congregationalists in Colonial Massachusetts.* Oxford: Oxford University Press, 1999.

Dunning, Albert E. *Congregationalists in America.* New York: J.A. Hill and Co., 1894.

Wesley, Alice Blair. *Our Covenant: The Lay and Liberal Doctrine of the Church.* Chicago: Meadville Lombard Theological School Press, 2002.

Wright, Conrad. *Walking Together: Polity and Participation in Unitarian Universalist Churches.* Boston: Skinner House, 1989.

WEBSITES

www.congregationallibrary.org/about/learning-more, bibliography on history of American Congregationalism

www.ucc.org/beliefs/theology/the-cambridge-platform-and.html, links to essays for 350th anniversary of Cambridge Platform

www.uua.org/uuhs/UUresources/minns5.html, Alice Blair Wesley's Minns Lecture on the Cambridge Platform